CHOICES AND CHANGES

Other Books by Joyce Slayton Mitchell

THE GUIDE TO COLLEGE LIFE

THE GUIDE TO CANADIAN UNIVERSITIES

OTHER CHOICES FOR BECOMING A WOMAN

FREE TO CHOOSE: DECISION MAKING FOR YOUNG MEN

WHAT'S WHERE: THE OFFICIAL GUIDE TO COLLEGE MAJORS

STOPOUT! WORKING WAYS TO LEARN

THE CLASSROOM TEACHER'S WORKBOOK FOR CAREER EDUCATION

SEE ME MORE CLEARLY: CAREER AND LIFE PLANNING FOR TEENS WITH PHYSICAL DISABILITIES

BE A MOTHER AND MORE: CAREER AND LIFE PLANNING

TAKING ON THE WORLD: EMPOWERING STRATEGIES FOR PARENTS OF CHILDREN WITH DISABILITIES

I CAN BE ANYTHING: A CAREER BOOK FOR WOMEN

HOW TO MAKE ENDS MEET: CREATIVE JOBS FOR RETIREMENT, *in press*

COMPUTER-AGE JOBS: THE COMPLETE GUIDE TO TECHNICAL AND BUSINESS CAREERS, *in press*

Choices and Changes

A Career Book for Men

Joyce Slayton Mitchell

NEW YORK, 1982
COLLEGE ENTRANCE EXAMINATION BOARD

Copies of this book may be ordered from:
College Board Publications Orders
Box 886
New York, NY 10101
The price is $9.95.

Editorial inquiries concerning this book should be directed to:
Editorial Office
The College Board
888 Seventh Avenue
New York, NY 10106

Library of Congress Catalog Number: 82–72389

Printed in the United States of America

9 8 7 6 5 4 3 2 1

CONTENTS

BUSINESS: COMPUTER OPERATIONS

BUSINESS: MONEY MANAGEMENT

BUSINESS: SALES

COMMUNICATIONS

EDUCATION

GOVERNMENT

HEALTH

SCIENCE AND TECHNOLOGY

SOURCES AND ACKNOWLEDGMENTS

The primary sources of information for **Choices and Changes** are career men in every part of the country and the 1982–83 edition of the *Occupational Outlook Handbook,* published by the United States Department of Labor. In addition to hundreds of personal and written interviews with working men, other examples of models were cited, with credit, from *Forbes, Fortune, The Wall Street Journal,* and various trade magazines.

It is a pleasure to thank the many contributors to this book: working men who told what work is like in their careers; Sandra MacGowan, Editor, The College Board, who worked so conscientiously on the manuscript; Sue Wetzel Gardner, Director of Publishing, and Jean Yoder, Managing Editor, The College Board, for their enthusiasm about this book; and Linda Magoon, typist and neighbor.

Wolcott, Vermont
August 1982

WARNING!

Job Opportunities Keep Changing!
Minorities Are Still in the Back of the Bus!
Unearned Income Counts, Too!

JOB OPPORTUNITIES KEEP CHANGING

Not even the United States Department of Labor can make foolproof predictions about what the future demand will be for jobs in any field. Predictions that the Department of Labor makes have to be based on particular economic and social assumptions, and these assumptions are always changing. For the past several years, the job future for college graduates has been poor and unemployment rates have been high. Besides unemployment, underemployment is at an all-time high in the 1980s. College graduates are underemployed when they wait on table, tend bar, pack groceries, or hold word-processing jobs that do not require a degree but provide ways to earn money until they find jobs related to their degrees and qualifications. When you realize that thousands of teachers and psychologists are still being prepared in spite of the scarcity of job openings, you will want to think about how you will find work if you are considering a teaching or counseling career.

As you read the career sections in this book, remember that predictions about the job futures in particular careers are based on the fact that the U.S. economy in the 1980s, so far, has been in a recession.

For the present, the good news about your job future is that some fields, such as accounting, nursing, engineering, and computer science, *are* continuing to grow, and that chances for your future employment in these fields are excellent.

MINORITIES ARE STILL IN THE BACK OF THE BUS

As you look at and read career information, be aware that, like most books and materials, they are stereotyped by sex and race. That is, the pictures are mostly of white boys and men, and the pronouns are "he" and "him." Therefore, get the information you need, but if you are black and interested in becoming a forester, a senator, a pilot, an astronaut, or perhaps a stockbroker, where less than 3 percent employed are nonwhite, don't expect these readings to encourage you to pursue such careers.

Racism and sexism, both in education and in employment, are against the law. But in a society where white males are considered "normal" and everyone else must adapt as best they can, racism and sexism are practiced both at school and at work. Getting a job, getting equal pay for equal work, getting promoted, and getting laid off are easy ways to measure how discrimination works. In all cases, minorities are at the lowest end of the scale, with unemployment figures being the highest for minority teenagers.

Even though there is a wider gap between men's and women's salaries, there also is a large gap between salaries for blacks and whites. In 1981, the average annual salary for white college graduates employed full-time was $11,400, compared with $10,400 for blacks.

Laws governing employment and education are now on the side of minorities. But, in order to test the law or to push for compliance with the law, minorities must aspire to and go after careers traditionally followed by whites, such as conservationist, pilot, real estate agent, stockbroker, and sales representative. If that's where your interests lie, be prepared to stand alone, and also be prepared to bring your friends with you into these well-paid, interesting fields, where everyone has a right to be.

UNEARNED INCOME COUNTS, TOO

Young men spend a lot of time and energy planning how to make money, but some don't realize the potential of putting their earned money to work for them through investments.

The goal of *Choices and Changes* is to help men achieve economic independence in a meaningful career. An important aspect of achieving economic independence is to understand what is meant by *invested income,* sometimes called *unearned income.* Unearned income means the interest you earn on your money.

Ask yourself these questions: Is your money working as hard for you as you are? Is your money invested at the best interest rate available? Or do you keep some money in a non-interest checking account and other money in a 5.5% savings account, as inflation eats it up with a double-digit bite? Is your money invested in ways that shelter income from taxes so that you are keeping the largest amount of dollars that you earn? You don't have to earn a huge salary before you learn to manage your money well. It's just as important to make your money work for you at $10,000 a year as it is at $50,000 a year.

Have you invested in an Individual Retirement Account (IRA)? Only since January 1, 1982, has *everyone* who earns $2,000 become eligible to contribute $2,000 tax-free each year to an IRA account. Saving $2,000 tax-free each year while it gathers tax-free interest is about the best investment deal most people ever get. Here is how it can work for you. If you start at 25 years old, you will retire with over *one and a half million dollars* ($1,718,284.21), based on a 12% annual assumed rate of return. If you are 35 years old and start your IRA plan now, at 65 you will have one-half million dollars ($540,585.21). And even if you are in the group of us who will start our IRA at 50 years old, you can retire in fifteen years with $83,309.56.

There are all kinds of ways to invest your money. One more way is a new salary-reduction plan that permits saving up to 10% of your pretax income a year to accumulate tax-free earnings until age 59½. But, whatever your age, unearned income is worth thinking about as you plan your career and finances. If you haven't heard investment language before, don't let it frighten you away. There are many good books you can read about investment and money management. A good one to start with is *The Only Investment Guide You'll Ever Need,* by Andrew Tobias. When you get some sense of your investment possibilities, talk with an accountant. Be a man who knows that good money management is crucial to economic independence.

CHOICES AND CHANGES!

How can you decide what you are going to be when you don't even know all the things there are to be? How can you decide what you are going to be when you aren't sure how much you like to do the things you've heard about? It's difficult to commit yourself to a career decision at this time in your life when you aren't at all sure how your values and priorities will change later.

For many young men, it is easier to think about what you don't want to be. For example, one thing you might be sure of is that you don't want to be a dentist like your father. Or you don't want to live in the town that your family lives in. Or you don't want to be tied down to a lifestyle that takes every cent you earn for a big family.

Your career decision should be easier if you realize that you *will* change jobs and directions for the sake of your career, as well as for other priorities in your life. You aren't choosing one career now to last you until your retirement. Just as your values and priorities have changed in the last five years, they will keep changing in the next five years and during the next twenty-five years. Look at the men of different ages whom you know—your cousins, uncles, neighbors, and friends. Think about them. Ask them what their priorities have been at different stages in their lives. Ask about the moves they may have made from one part of the country to another, the changes in their jobs, in their families, in the money they made and spent, and in their interests during different periods of their lives.

Just as you change with time, as a result of your experiences and the people you meet, the world of work changes, too. Years ago, a young man could plan for only one job or one career. But today, a young person can look forward to an average of seven different jobs, or seven "mini-careers," during his lifetime of work. For example, you may start out as a salesperson, go into management in a real estate agency, leave that job for a political appointment in your state government, venture into commercial real estate in a resort area, and expand into a job as recreational developer. Even then you may be open for several more changes before your work life is completed. Many young men in their twenties who were interviewed for this book are already in their second or third different job. Some are getting business training anywhere they can in order to get the experience they need to go into business for themselves. Others are making changes for higher-level jobs and more money. Still others are changing jobs to get a broader base of experience in business because they plan a management career in their future.

Something good happens to you if you realize that you aren't choosing the one and only right career for you—or the wrong career. Something good happens to you when you can use everything you experience to build what you eventually become. There is no way that you can know now, or even should know, what that will be.

Think of former President Jimmy Carter. He entered the work force with a military science career at Annapolis—a long way from his human rights focus as the President of the United States! He made a crucial decision to leave the military and his nuclear-submarine engineering career to go back to Georgia where he was born. There, he worked in the family peanut farm business. When he decided to enter politics and run for governor of his state, he used all the skills he had learned since he began working: self-discipline, logical thinking, compromise, business skills, local concerns, national concerns, communications. In other words, everything he did counted. And everything you do counts, too. There is no work or life experience that can't be used toward the career and life you end up with.

Some people don't analyze experience; they haven't learned to use it as consciously as Jimmy Carter has. In many articles about the former President, you may have noticed that one of his values is always to do the best job he can, to learn the most from it, and to apply what he learned to what he does next. He doesn't waste energy worrying about how he could have done a job better, or how he should have been working somewhere else, or working with someone else. He cashes in on everything he does. He learns from wherever he is, from whomever he is with. From the Presidency of the United States, we don't know what Jimmy Carter will do next. It can be interesting for you to watch and see what career his skills, experiences, values, and interests will take him to.

With the attitude that everything counts, and that choosing your career is a long process, it may be easier for you to see how your school or family work or present job and interests fit into this process. The subjects you study, the sports you play, music you listen to, jobs you hold, children you raise, friends you have, and test scores you get all add up to your career development. All of the decisions you make now are career decisions.

COLLEGE: A CAREER DECISION

At any age, deciding to go to college or back to college is a career decision. For young adults, choosing a college can be your first move away from home, and this move makes it different from career decisions you have made before this time. But, whether you live away from home or at home, choosing a college changes your life more than selecting Spanish IV or mathematics IV in high school.

Which College Should You Choose?

Does it make a difference where you go to college? Is it true graduates of some colleges get all the good bank and corporation training opportunities while others never have a chance? Does a photographer or an actor have to go to college? Each career description in ***Choices and Changes*** cites the necessary education needed for that career. You will read that business executives often come from a liberal arts background, pilots from military training, commercial artists from two-year professional art schools, psychologists from Ph.D. programs.

Deciding where to go to college is difficult because, like the job market, the college situation is changing too. Costs are soaring. Community colleges have mushroomed everywhere, and students continue to transfer, dropout, stopout, take college courses by examination or in the corporate world, and further their education in lifelong learning programs that educators and your parents never dreamed possible just a few years ago.

There are a lot of ways to select a college. One way is to choose the college closest to your home, where you know the most number of students. Another way is to choose a college that is recruiting the hardest for students. Many students select a college by a particular program offered, or because they have decided upon a particular career. Still another way to select a college is to make a systematic survey of all the universities and colleges available to you and to choose a few that have the most meaning for you. *When you get as much information about a college as the college gets about you, then you will have the basis for a good decision.*

Important factors to consider are a college's admission requirements, where the college is located, and how much it costs. It is also essential to understand in some detail what a college is like, and if it is a setting in which you are likely to achieve success. You must ask more than, "Can I get in?" You should also ask, "What will it be like *after* I get in?" Only then can you begin to ask yourself these questions:

- "What are the implications for me of one type of college life over another type?"
- "Will I be different if I go to a collegiate college, or an experimental college, or a technical college?"
- "What effect will one campus atmosphere have on my selection of friends, or possibly of spouse, and on my political, religious, and career values?"

A student choosing a college has much the same job as a college admission officer in selecting a student. From your record, the officer can look at your height, weight, age, college admission scores, and high school grades. However, until the admission officer meets you personally and reviews personality reports from your high school, he or she doesn't have a precise idea of who you really are.

Should You Choose According to Majors Offered?

What about selecting a college by a curriculum it offers? If you select a college for a particular field, look at offerings in several related programs rather than at a specific program. For example, if you are interested in chemistry now, you may end up in one of the physical sciences but not necessarily in chemistry. If you are like most students, you aren't quite sure yet what you want to be, or which major is best for you. Many courses that colleges offer will be completely new to you.

Students change. They change majors and they change colleges. Over 75 percent of all first-year college students leave the college they choose. That means that three out of four first-year students change the decision they made about their college choice. And the more specialized the school (engineering, business, architecture), the higher the rate of transfers and dropouts. In fact, 50 percent of all graduating *seniors* don't even go into work that is related to their major! With statistics such as these, you can easily see that selecting a college for its program may not be as good a reason to decide as it appears. If you are planning a four-year college program, the most helpful direction you can take right now is one of general exploration—not specialization—for the first year. After all, there are many majors and courses in college you haven't tried and maybe haven't even heard about, so it is difficult for you to know which ones you should choose before you go there.

For more information on college majors, read *What's Where: The Official Guide to College Majors* (J. S. Mitchell, New York: Avon, 1979) and the annual *Index of Majors* (New York: The College Board).

Consider the Transferable Skills You Can Learn

In choosing your college according to the programs it offers, remember one important fact: the world of work is *not* divided into college majors. Learning the transferable skills that people use over and over in many careers is the goal of the college student, whatever the major. For example, speaking, writing, decision making, time management, persistence, and persuasive skills can be learned in any college major, from philosophy to physical education to computer science. And keep in mind that half of all college students go into careers completely unrelated to their college major. This means that transferable skills are really what they are getting out of college. As you choose between a technical and a liberal arts program, think about what transferable skills you could learn in each program that you can use to your advantage in many work environments.

If you choose a liberal arts, or general, education, nothing will be more important than the transferable skills you will learn in that program. According to the President of Princeton University, Dr. William G. Bowen, "Some sensitivity to other people and their feelings, and a reasonable broad perspective on the world and its inhabitants, are of enormous value in many callings." President Bowen adds, "I am continually getting letters from representatives of leading business firms in New York who say, 'For the individuals we hire with a view to moving up into management we feel that the liberal arts degree is the most desirable fundamental preparation.' "

A Matter of Money

Money usually is a factor to consider when you choose a college. With a shrinking economy, severe cutbacks in government-funded student loans, and skyrocketing college costs, paying for a college education is more difficult to do than ever before. As you consider which colleges to apply to, read as much information as you can to get a realistic picture of what colleges cost today and ways that might be available to help you finance that cost.

Each year, The College Board publishes a step-by-step guide to financing a college education, called *The College Cost Book* (New York: The College Board). This book lists expenses at 3,200 schools and colleges and gives you directions for computing how much money a college might expect your parents or you to pay toward your educational expenses. It also provides information about financial aid programs and tells you exactly how and where to apply for them.

Another useful booklet with some creative ideas about how to pay for college costs is *The College Financial Aid Emergency Kit: The Best-ever Pocket Guide to Scholarships, Loans, and Other Remedies for Skinned-up, Broken-down, Wiped-out Budgets* (Sun Features, Inc., Box 368J, Cardiff, CA 92007).

After you find out how much each college you are applying to costs, and how much your family and you can afford to pay for your education, you will want to check further with the financial officer of each college. The college financial officer has the most up-to-date information about grants, aids, loans, and work programs. The financial officer also will be able to tell you about military and private industry tuition plans for college students. Once you are accepted in a college (and financial need is increasingly a factor in your acceptance), the college is usually very eager to find a way for you to pay.

Many students with financial need are led to believe that

they must qualify for loans, grants, or scholarships by having top grades or the highest rank in class. As you think about your college choice, it is crucial for you to know that most government grants and loans and many from colleges are based on financial need, not on academic merit. If you have the academic standards to get into a college, then you have enough merit for the college to award help with your finances. If you are an older college applicant who has worked for a few years, whether for the work experience or because you needed to earn money, your age cannot influence whether or not you receive financial aid. In other words, if you need the money, regardless of your test scores, or rank in class, or age, or sex, or race, *ask* about financial aid!

Today, many students are trying to keep their college expenses down by enrolling in less expensive community college programs where they can live at home at a much lower cost, rather than choosing a residential public or private college that can cost as much as $10,000 a year. If you are headed for an advanced degree or a professional school after four years of college, such as medicine, law, business, or education, you may want to save money by going to a community college nearby your home for your basic liberal arts training.

Consider the Saleable Skills You Can Learn

Because of the tremendous cost of colleges and the changing college employment market, you may decide not to make the capital investment in a four-year college. If you aren't enthusiastic about studying and learning academic subjects, chances are that four years in college may not be worth it for you financially, especially in terms of the few available jobs when you graduate. Instead, you may choose to go to a community college for a two-year program in a technical or business field that will teach you the saleable skills for a specific job with good employment possibilities, such as computer science, technical engineering, or technical health care.

With a little planning ahead, you can learn saleable skills in a four-year liberal arts college, too. Planning can save you the trouble and expense of having to learn these skills after graduation. Even if you select a major in Japanese religion or Russian literature because of your interest, it can be developed toward a paying career. If you add a few courses to your Japanese religion and Russian literature curriculums that help you acquire saleable skills, such as word processing, accounting, or basic computer programming, it may mean the difference between getting a job that requires a college degree when you graduate or not getting such a job. Or you may see the tie-in between business and Russian or Japanese studies in a broader sense, and then use your original academic interest in a practical way in your career.

Take Andrew Tobias as an example. While at Harvard, he majored in Slavic languages and literature, but his main activity was earning money to help pay for his tuition. He worked for a student agency that provided various services, from bartending to computer training. By his senior year, he became President of the agency. During that time, he created a popular book for students: *How To Earn A Lot of Money in College.* He used his earning experience while in college to get a job with The National Student Marketing Corporation, and his latest publishing ventures are best-selling books about finance, investments, and insurance. Tobias got a liberal arts education, but he learned saleable and transferable skills while he was in college in order to pay for that education.

College students who don't plan ahead toward employment often must return to school, at added expense and time, to learn a saleable skill. A University of Michigan graduate who had majored in anthropology couldn't find a job related to his major. He then took a one-year course in X-ray technology in order to have a part-time job that he could live on while he went to graduate school—which still did not guarantee him a job in anthropology when he graduated! Another young man with a Ph.D. in education, and without a job related to his training in sight, earned a certificate in emergency medical technology. He now drives an ambulance part-time while he writes a book he thinks will help him compete for the kind of job he wants five years from now.

No matter what your subject interest, think about ways you can learn one or more saleable skills before you graduate. Consider how these practical skills can be combined with your subject interest to make it more marketable in the career world. This will give you that competitive edge in the job market over other applicants.

Should You Choose According to Campus Life?

The college guides suggested on page 15 will give you an idea of how one college is different from another. When you compare the rules of various colleges, you will learn about their attitudes toward student responsibilities and college authority. You will get an idea of campus character and personality. Remember, however, that the kind of campus life a college offers does not indicate its academic standards for admission. You can't tell how difficult it is to get into a college by the number of hours the library is open. You don't have to be a superior student to find a college with an intellectual atmosphere where much of the academic responsibility is given to the student. And the reverse is true. Many colleges that accept only above-average and superior students provide a social and sports-oriented atmosphere rather than an intellectual one, with little academic responsibility given to the students.

Whatever the quality of a college campus, you must relate it to your own expectations of what college life will be like. Look for the type of campus environment you think will be most successful and most productive for you. Find a setting that gives you a chance to try out your interests and abilities, one that gives you the kind of support and encouragement you need. For example, if you don't have a sister, and have very few female friends, you may find that co-ed living makes you too uptight to cope academically. Or you may decide that learning to live and work among women is a top personal priority for you right now. You must relate your findings about differences in college life to yourself. These findings have no meaning for anyone else. As you look around at your friends, you can see that some of them will want a very different type of campus life than you want. Ask yourself these questions:

- "To what degree can I accept academic and social responsibility?"
- "How much responsibility do I take *now* for my life?"
- "How strict are my parents' rules compared to the college's rules?"
- "In what kinds of classroom climate do I work the hardest?"

- "How do the colleges I'm looking at relate to what I know about myself and the degree of responsibility I accept?"

Try to answer these questions about yourself as you find out what campus life is like at various colleges.

What about Prestige?

Many students do not think about the prestige of a college until they are already attending the college. Then they begin to hear about their college's prestige—or lack of it.

What does *prestige* mean, anyway? It means having a well-known reputation for being one of the best. Sometimes prestige is misleading. A college can have a great reputation in its own state, or even in its own region, but not be nationally well-known. For example, Denison University in Ohio is a prestigious liberal arts college in the Midwest. But few students on the East or West coasts would consider it equal to Oberlin, also in Ohio but better known nationally. A university can get its prestige from its medical school or its graduate school in business, and yet its undergraduate school, where you will be heading, may be very ordinary and have classes taught by graduate students rather than by fully qualified professors. Ohio State and other "Big Ten" colleges get their prestige from their football teams, but the quality of the football team has little to do with a university's academic standards.

Hundreds of colleges may have the academic program, the campus environment, and other advantages you are looking for. Prestige may or may not add to fulfilling your requirements for a college. The point to be made here is that it's helpful for you to know about the prestige of a college (determined by a great variety of factors), but the most prestigious college may not necessarily be the best college for you.

If you are choosing among Amherst, Swarthmore, University of Chicago, and the local state college—and you have the money and grades for all four—go to the private college with the prestige. College can be where you begin to build your network of friends who will keep you tuned in to new career opportunities as you advance. If money or your academic record or geography keep you out, and you long for a degree from prestigious Brown, MIT, Harvard, or Stanford, then you can always apply later as a transfer or graduate student. Other than medicine and law, many graduate schools are easier to get into than their undergraduate colleges.

College Guides to Choosing

There are many kinds of college guides, and your high school guidance officer will certainly have the basic ones. Read the college descriptions in the guides to find out about the options available to you in higher education. In them you can learn about student enrollment, the size of the community where the college is located, the programs offered, the cost, the level of competition for admission, the social clubs on campus, the quality of student life. Three basic and complete college guides are *The College Handbook* (New York: The College Board); *Comparative Guide to American Colleges* (J. Cass and M. Birnbaum, New York: Harper & Row); and *The New American Guide to Colleges* (G. R. Hawes and P. N. Novalis, New York: New American Library). One other college guide, written by *Yale Daily News* students, is *The Insider's Guide to the Colleges* (New York: Putnam).

THE FOCUS IS ON YOU

Choosing a college, a major field of study, and a career are not easy decisions for anyone to make. One way to help decide what you are going to do is to focus your attention away from the outside pressures and back onto yourself. You don't have to concentrate immediately on a school's expectation of you, your career education, the world of work, possible prejudices and sex-role stereotypes, the inflated economy, and the changing labor market. All of these things will be factors in your eventual decision, but what you need right now is to explore your career possibilities, no matter what conditions exist or what changes might take place.

You've Got Loads of Career Possibilities

There are hundreds of jobs in every field for you to investigate. You can work full-time. Or you may wish to share a job and use the rest of your time to write, make furniture, or raise a child. You may want to work part-time, or volunteer some of your time. Or you may want to create your own job.

Some men choose their career only by the opportunity it gives them to make money—even though some of their personal interests are not met in their work. By making the money they need, they free themselves to use their leisure time for self-fulfillment in other ways. For example, Kelly M. Alexander, Jr., Vice President of the North Carolina NAACP Youth Division, tells young men: "Get an economic base that will make you independent, then branch out. Indulge your secret desire to be an artist, a politician, or whatever appeals to you. I make my living not as a writer but in the funeral business. Nevertheless, I don't limit myself to just that business. I also write magazine articles on topics as diverse as the desegregation of the Boston schools and career choices for young black men. I'm active in the NAACP on the local, state, and national levels; worked in statewide political campaigns; and conducted successful voter registration drives. I have an A.B. degree in political science and an M.A. in public administration. It has been important to me always to take jobs that gave me enough economic security to be able to be independent, but also left me with enough flexibility to do the other things I like to do." Alexander urges nonwhites not to become thoughtless consumers of whatever "the Joneses" happen to have. "Don't want something or do something simply because the white kids have it or are doing it. Ask yourself whether or not it is necessary, or whether you could do without it. What price do you have to pay to get it? You be the judge of how much you want to pay. I, for one, have turned down good paying jobs in places like New York and Washington, D.C., because I like the people and the trees of my native North Carolina. I decided not to go to graduate school at Kansas, Syracuse, or George Washington because I didn't feel like moving. My decisions are counter to the dominant ethic of my many black friends, but that's the way I wanted to work things out for me."

Other men choose careers that become everything to them—their very lives. They love every part of their work, and every spare moment goes into it. Their hobby *is* their work. They are never off-duty. For example, a bookstore owner spends his vacations in other bookstores, a writer views everything in terms of how it fits into stories, a car salesperson notices who is driving what car model, and a businessman works 80 hours some weeks to plan every detail as he wants it. Top manager Victor Palmieri, who specializes in the management of troubled assets, is this kind of man. He is the son of Italian immigrants and was raised in a poor neighborhood in California. He won a scholarship to Stanford University. After Stanford Law School, he joined a law firm for a short period, then went into real estate where he became a developer. After four years of constant work as president of the real estate company, he developed it into a resort business by buying Sun Valley. Still only in his midthirties, he left the real estate business when the U.S. government asked him to conduct a study of the causes of urban riots. Rethinking his career direction after his year in Washington, D.C., he went into business for himself. He found that making money was exciting and easy, and he put all of his energy into troubled businesses. He joined the ailing Great Southwestern Railroad for $25,000 a month. When he had successfully managed the company and Great Southwestern became an ongoing business, the Penn Central Railroad hired him as a specialist in crisis management. His fee for five years was $21 million, plus benefits and extras. Palmieri and his wife were separated after 25 years of marriage. The time he spent at work was undoubtedly a factor in the separation. Now he spends some weekend time with his three sons. Victor Palmieri is a millionaire with a career he loves. One can safely say that his work is his life.

Palmieri's case is an extreme one. Most of you will develop your career in ways that bring a balance to your life and that suit your own personality and values. This balance will include your job, your family and friends, your volunteer work, your sports, and hobbies. And the balance will *change.* Family, promotions, and midlife changes will add transition and will offset the balance, which always must be managed.

Today people have more options for career choices and lifestyles than at any time in this country's history. You can choose to earn the money you need on your own, or to let a partner take the major responsibility for making money while you do something else—or any career arrangement in between. Focus first on *you* and the kind of life you want, and next on jobs, as you make your choices and changes to develop your career.

Male Expectations

Traditionally, a young man's focus in choosing a career has been very different than the focus of a young woman. The young man is expected to financially support himself plus others when he grows up. The young woman is expected to be financially supported when she grows up. You have been programmed to measure yourself as a person who counts most according to the amount of money you make. She has been programmed to count most according to the amount of money her husband makes. You have been programmed as a "success object." She has been programmed as a "sex object." The more you understand how you are systematically set up for certain choices, the more you will see a chance to vary those choices.

A "New Age" for Young Men

In her book *Passages,* Gail Sheehy describes the possibility of a "new age" for young men. She writes about new life patterns for men, and one of those patterns is the "integrator." In this life pattern, men would try to integrate their families, including child care, with their ambitions and their career development, as they also attempt to balance the money they make with what will benefit society. Men would consider the human costs of specific career decisions: how a promotion might take time away from their families, how a move might affect their wives' career development, how a business risk would influence their families' independence. An "integrator," or a young man in a new age, would be quite different from the traditional or stereotyped man, who makes career and family decisions and commitments in his twenties and never strays from them.

It's easy to see how young men become victims of the stereotype, and it's crucial for you to know how you have been programmed, ever since you were asked the question, "What are you going to be when you grow up?" Your young answer was probably, "a cowboy," "a fireman," or "an astronaut." Adults don't stop pressing little boys about what they are going to be until little boys actually become "something." And in school, most elementary schoolbooks picture adult men continually at work. In fact, adult men are so hard at work that the impression school children get is that the only purpose in life for a man is to assume the total financial responsibility for his family by working.

When you finally get into high school, you are often counseled as if the only goal of your education is to transform you into an economic commodity. You prepare yourself in school as an economic investment going after the maximum profit. Many teachers and parents are not always conscious of the fact that they are preparing you to be a "success object." They say that you should take a strong academic program, with an emphasis on math and science, leading to a profession or business career that makes a lot of money or is prestigious. Of course, they will say, everyone is different, each person is an individual, but by advising you in the way they do, they are unconsciously encouraging you to become a male stereotype. Most educators assume that a man will put his career first; his friendships and marriage don't count as much to him and will just "fall naturally into place" in the part of his life not occupied by his career. It's assumed that if a man is very successful, he won't be bothered by poor personal relationships anyway. The unspoken assumption is that primarily you must be an achiever and provider, rather than a person who can choose to integrate your work life with your personal life.

But in the new age for men, you can begin to see yourself developing as a whole person with many choices, rather than as a man who has to earn more than anyone else, who has to control and dominate all relationships, and who has to successfully compete with his peers. In the new age, you don't have to be a success object. You can be successful at many things, not just making money; but of course you can choose to be successful at that, too. You can be successful in your work, with your friends, with your family, in the community, in arts and music, in sports, and in other hobbies. In the new age, you have a chance to work through your own values to develop your own lifestyle. You don't have to define yourself only as the breadwinner and measure yourself as a "real man" by the amount of money you make. You can consider *sharing* the stress and responsibility of a breadwinner. You can consider making major changes.

In the new age, you can look forward to an equal partnership with your wife. As equal partners, you may both decide what each of you will do. Cooking, making money, rearing children, painting the house, cutting the grass, doing the laundry, and more are all necessary for the partnership to function. Equal partnership doesn't mean you both have to paint the house or raise the children; it does mean you decide who will do what on the basis of who is best at it, or who has the most time and interest in the job, or who hates it the least, instead of deciding on the basis of being male or female. Equal partnership doesn't mean you are both the same, or even that you could be the same. It means that you both have equal opportunity and equal responsibility to decide about rearing the children, about buying the food, about making money, and about all the choices and changes that create a full life.

When you understand the new age for men, you won't be tied to the idea of measuring a man according to how much money he makes or how prestigious his job is. In the new age, you can consider all career possibilities on the basis of your interests, your abilities, your hopes and dreams, and your ambitions. You don't have to concentrate and specialize too soon, as if your only purpose in work is to get to the top first. You can *change* careers as your interests change, and you can redirect yourself as you grow. You can relate your career to your family life. For the first time, you can say, "Wait a minute! That's not for me. I'm not like all males, I'm not a stereotype. I don't have to make the most money to count." You can discover who you are as an individual, and you can work out your career with a partner, who can help you support each other and your family. In this new age, you can be free to explore all kinds of career directions that are unique for you—and the kind of life *you* want to live.

Develop Your Career

There are three basic steps in your career development. The first is to learn about yourself—to assess your own skills, values, and interests. The second is to learn about work—to locate your career possibilities. And the third step is to find the educational pathways that will lead you to where you want to go.

What Skills Can You Call Your Own?

The purpose of your education is to learn what you like to do and how well you can do it. At the same time, you learn what you don't like and what you don't do well. For example, in the classroom you learn how much mathematics and foreign language you can master. In addition to learning such content skills, you also learn transferable skills—how well you read, study, speak, and write. You apply these skills to all the subjects you learn and also to all career situations.

You learn what your skills are not only by grades, test scores, pay, and promotions, but also by your own evaluation. Although your school grades may predict how well you will do in college, they don't necessarily measure all the skills you have learned. You can't possibly tell what you are going to accomplish in life merely by your school grades and achievements. For example, if you rank fourth in your mathematics class right now, that doesn't mean that you will be fourth in money-making ability in your age group twenty years from now. Grades in high school and college *do not* predict who will be happiest, most miserable, richest, poorest, or most powerful, either in work or in family life.

To find out more about your skills, take a look at your everyday actions—not only what you say you like or don't like, but the things you actually *do* with your time. Think about the subjects you study in school, the tasks you perform at work, the things you do at home that really excite you, that make you feel special and make the time run fast. Notice what activities make you feel good, and what activities make you feel lousy and make you feel you can't wait to get them over with. Think about how your activities are related to having fun, to making money, to school or work or community achievement. Then, notice what skills are needed for the activities you love. Is time-management one of them? Is decision-making important? Is being your own boss and taking the initiative a part of your enjoyment? Do you get along with almost anyone, or much more with one group of people than another? Do your activities involve getting others to participate with you? Do they involve staying with a project after you've lost your initial enthusiasm? Here are a few more pertinent questions:

- Do you prefer to work in a particular situation or location?
- Do you prefer to work with particular types of people?
- Is money your main goal? Is power?
- Do you think you would like a job that is short on money but long on prestige?
- Would you like a job where you can be left to work on your own? Would you like to be your own boss?
- What kind of physical surroundings do you prefer where you work?
- Do you mind traveling, or working occasionally at night and on weekends?

As you learn about yourself, you will notice how you relate to others. You will discover your ability to get along with other students, your family, and your co-workers; your leadership abilities in class and on the job; and your ability to get along with authority, such as your boss, your teachers, your coach, and your parents. Of course, your skills, interests, and values will change. In fact, many work and school experiences often bring about major changes in how you feel and act. But even bearing these changes in mind, you still can learn a lot right now about your skills in school, at home, and at work.

Reading Tells You a Lot about a Career

Choices and Changes: A Career Book for Men is about work. The "career clusters" in this book describe many different jobs and career possibilities. Read about several careers that sound as if they describe your interests. When one career in a cluster interests you, read about the occupations related to it as well. Using the clusters in this way may help you find new ideas.

Sometimes people in a business-oriented family tend to look only at business careers, or people with relatives working in the military or government tend to examine only those fields. Or perhaps someone in your family has told you "you ought to be" a business man, or a dentist, or a new car dealer, and you may not like the idea. You may reject it before you seriously consider whether the career is a good one for you or not. Explore career possibilities that *you* have in mind, not those your family or friends say you should look at or not look at. After researching these possibilities, you'll either want to learn more about them or will be able safely to eliminate those possibilities.

As you research the careers in ***Choices and Changes,*** notice that the average salaries are cited for each career. It is easy to think of the average as the exact salary at which you can expect to start working. For example, in 1981 engineers with a bachelor's degree started at an average of $22,900. What that average figure really means is that some engineers started at $18,900 a year while others started at $26,900. Beginning engineers *averaged* $22,900. For a better idea of the money you can expect in a particular career, you will want to translate the average salary into a range of starting salaries. Within this range, the particular salary you start with will depend on the college you attended, your college record, your work experience, where the job is located, and the type of employer.

If you are a student now, salaries will be even higher by the time you are ready for the job market because of inflation and cost-of-living salary increases. To give you an idea of the future rate of increase, let's look at past salaries for teachers. In 1976, teachers averaged $11,700; in 1981, they averaged $17,725. Remember, when you read "average," that means many workers make less and just as many may make more than the figure cited.

As you choose a career, what does money mean to you? Will your income be high enough to maintain the standard of living you want and justify your education costs? How much will your earnings increase as you gain experience? Like most people, you probably think of "salary" as money. But money is only one type of financial reward for work. Paid vacations, holidays, and sick leave; life, health, and accident insurance; and retirement and pension plans are also part of the total earnings package. Some employers also offer stock options and profit-sharing plans, savings plans, and bonuses.

Which jobs pay the most? This is a difficult question to answer because good information is available only for one type of earnings—wages. Obviously, some kinds of work pay better than others. But, many times, the same kind of work does not always pay the same amount of money. Some areas of the country offer better pay than others for the same type of work. For example, the average weekly earnings of a beginning computer programmer vary from city to city. Generally, earnings are higher in the North Central and Northeast regions of the country than in the West and South. You should also remember that cities that offer the highest earnings are often those in which it is most expensive to live.

Earnings for the same type of work also vary according to the type of organization you work for. For example, Ph.D. chemists in marketing and production earn more than Ph.D. chemists in industrial research and development; however, those in industrial research earn more than chemistry professors, who also must do research.

Undoubtedly you will wonder what the economy will be like when you enter the labor market. Each career description anticipates your chances for getting a job through the 1980s. These chances are estimates developed by the U.S. Department of

Labor, and they are based on the following general assumptions about the future of the economy and the country:

- Energy prices will not rise dramatically to alter the growth of the Gross National Product (GNP).
- The institutional framework of the U.S. economy will not change radically.
- Current social, technological, and scientific trends will continue.
- No major events, such as widespread or long-lasting energy shortages or war, will significantly alter the rates of industrial and economic growth.
- Federal grants-in-aid to state and local governments will decline.
- Federal expenditures will decline as a proportion of the Gross National Product.

Finally, you should remember that job prospects in your community or state may not correspond to the description of employment outlook given here. The outlook in your area may be better—or worse—for the particular job you are interested in. The local office of your State Employment Service is the best place to ask about employment projections in your area.

Looking at all the possibilities, then, find one or two or three careers that sound interesting enough to read about and research further. Reading in detail about a career is a reliable way to acquire accurate information about that career. Some people make their choices only on information provided by the mass media. A detective or doctor or trial lawyer on television often produces a romantic picture of his or her career. None of the beginning drudgery and dirty work that all jobs demand, nor the long hours away from the family, may come through in a television or otherwise stereotyped version of a career.

After reading the career descriptions that interest you, write to the professional groups cited for more information. Look in your school library for some of the recommended readings listed for each job, or send away for readings if your library does not carry them. Notice in particular the trade magazines cited for each career. If you want the inside story of what people in a career are reading, thinking about, and actually doing, read their trade magazine! *The Wall Street Journal, Variety,* and *Veterinary Economics* are where you will find out what the financial, theater, and vet people are really like. It isn't academic theory but the business of the job itself that you'll find in the trade magazines. In addition to learning what people in a field are doing, you can't beat the trade magazine as raw material for a job interview. For example, nothing will impress a book publisher more than hearing you discuss facts about his or her business you acquired from reading *Publishers Weekly;* or a physician, if you can talk about the latest research published in the *New England Journal of Medicine;* or a banker, if you have the latest economy reports from the *American Banker;* or an urban planner, if you are aware of recent urban trends in *City.* If your school library doesn't have the trade magazines you are interested in, check your community library or a local college library. For those of you who don't have a library resource, publishing addresses are cited at the end of each career description. Write for one issue to find out what's going on in the fields you are considering.

What Do Others Think about Their Work?

Talking to people who are willing to discuss their work is an excellent way to find out about a career you are interested in. One good place to find people to interview about their work is in your own family. Ask your parents, aunts, uncles, and their friends to help you find some people who are already in the career you are thinking about entering. Talk with those people. If a securities salesperson is what you want to be, find a stockbroker and ask him what it's like to be in securities. Does it sound like you? Ask another person what it's like to be in that field. How much of the job does he really like? What parts of the job does he hate and wish were over as soon as he starts them? Listen to everything you hear from others as it relates to you, because *you* are the one who will be selling and either enjoying the hustle and competition or getting an ulcer by the time you finally make the sale. Let others you talk to know about your interest in their work.

In addition to your family, many of your teachers or coworkers will be good sources for finding people in careers that you are ready to research. Clergy, youth-group leaders, and many people in your community, including the alumni from your school, will want to help with career development. Some of them already have specific programs to help, while others are looking for ways to help. Ask them if they know a forester, a computer systems analyst, or a foreign service officer you can meet and interview in your career research. Don't wait until you are choosing a college major or hunting for a job to talk with others about their work. The more experience you have talking with people in careers that interest you, the more background you'll have for your decisions ahead. Not only will your interview experiences be good training for future interviews, they will also have value right now in teaching you more about work and the ways that work will fit into your life.

Even if you don't know someone, but you have read about his or her interesting work in the paper, go ahead and write to that person, saying that you are interested in learning about his or her job or in working with the person during the summer or school holiday. Usually, people are flattered about your interest. In this way, you can learn how to make your own opportunities for future interviews and jobs. Students are in a good position for exploring. You have a positive image, and people aren't threatened that you will take over their job. So, make the most of your learning status to learn about careers from the people already doing well in them.

When you have the names of people to interview, call them. Tell them you would like to talk with them for a specific amount of time, so they will know you won't keep them too long from their work. Say, for instance, that you are interested in being a computer programmer and want to talk about what the job is like with someone who knows. Ellen J. Wallach, career-development specialist, suggests that you make an appointment, then have the following questions in mind to help begin the interview:

- How did you get into this career?
- How did you view the work before you got into it? Is your view different now? How is it different?
- What do you like *most* about your work?
- What do you like *least* about your work?
- Why did you choose this type of work?

- What are the greatest pressures, strains, and anxieties about your work?
- What special problems might someone new to the job have in adjusting to it?
- Would you make the same career choice again? Why?
- Besides the environment in which you work, where else could someone perform your work?
- Are there careers related to your work?
- How much time do you spend with your family? Is this amount what you expected to spend when you began working in this career?
- How much time do you spend with hobbies?
- How do your family and friends fit into the lifestyle of your career?
- What are the greatest "highs" about this work—what really turns you on about it?

At the end of the interview, advises Wallach, always ask the following questions: "Is there anyone else you know who also does your kind of work who might be willing to speak to me? May I use your name when I call?" And when you get home, write a short thank-you note to the worker for sharing his or her time and work with you. This follow-up is a must.

Throughout your career-research process, remember that everything you learn counts. Even though you decide that a given career isn't what you had thought it was before your research, you are still ahead to have the accurate information. You may learn about new careers indirectly, and your follow-up from reading and interviews may lead you in directions you didn't plan on taking. The more information you finally have for your career decision, the more sure you can be of your decision—at least for this phase in your life.

Test Your Interest through Work Experience

Choosing and changing work experiences are pathways or directions toward your career development. Actual work experience provides opportunities where you can try out your school knowledge in a work situation.

Once you get a career idea that makes sense for you, use your summer vacation, after-school time, and weekends for a trial run in that career, whether it's paid work or volunteer work. Work at a car agency if you are interested in sales, or in a hospital if you are interested in health care. Work with a children's group in a day camp or child-care center if you are interested in education, or in a bookstore or publishing house if the book business interests you. Try a summer job in a bank or real estate office if finance is your interest.

Even though the kind of work you are likely to get is the lowest level in that field and, therefore, reserved for beginners, the menial tasks become meaningful if you apply what you learn to your own career development. Even if you are doing a repetitious job that takes no thinking, you can look around at the whole system and notice what the next step up is for people who have permanent jobs and can get promotions. Who is your boss? Who is his boss? Who is the top boss? Do any of those jobs look interesting? For example, a summer job in a real estate office may consist of painting front doors on homes to be sold. But you can look around and see the hours kept by other salespeople, listen to the kinds of questions clients ask and the answers salespeople give, and notice which salespeople are making the most money, which are putting in the most time, and which are living a life you would like to live.

Getting ahead in a job is like learning to walk or to ski. You've got to put so many hours and so many miles into the learning, no matter who you are, or how fit you are, or how well-qualified you are. When you start summer work, or an after-school job, or your first full-time job, you will probably start at the bottom. Setting goals is what people do who really want to get ahead. It's especially important when you just begin a job and it turns out that the job isn't everything you had hoped it would be.

Curt Carlson, Chairman and President of one of the nation's largest privately owned businesses, went from $85 a month to owning a business that makes $1 billion in sales. All this happened, he claims, because he is a goal-setter. When he started working, he wrote down what his next goal would be on a piece of paper and put it in his wallet. Once he reached that goal, he replaced the slip of paper with another one. His first goal was to make $100 a week. Carlson worked part of his way through the University of Minnesota by selling soap. After two years of noticing who was buying what products and which sales were up, he borrowed $50 to start his own company, a trading-stamp company for grocery stores. He worked at it for thirteen years before his first break came when he signed up his first large grocery chain. Since that time, he has taken on many new businesses and set hundreds of new goals. Carlson says, "I believe that you should never be content with reaching a goal." What's on his slip of paper in his wallet now that he has reached $1 billion? $2 billion in the next year!

Your work may not always seem related to where you want to end up. But when you see how everything about a job counts, then your present work activity takes on new meaning. When the apprentice architect understands how he can use his training to get ahead, then the tedious job of drafting other peoples ideas becomes more meaningful. Your purpose in career exploration and development is to help you determine all the possible choices and changes you can make for your future.

Another work alternative, besides summer jobs and after-school work, is an internship or voluntary program for an academic year in place of going to college. An internship is a supervised work experience where the student can learn about a career or field of interest. Usually the student is not paid, but often he or she can earn college credit. Many students "stop out" of school for a year after high school or after their first year of college to test a career idea. A basic guide for internships during the academic years is *Stopout! Working Ways to Learn* (J. S. Mitchell, available from Garrett Park Press, Garrett Park, MD 20766). For summer internships, read the annual *National Directory of Summer Internships for Undergraduate College Students* (Bryn Mawr and Haverford College, by M. E. Updike and M. E. Rivera, available from Career Planning Office, Haverford College, Haverford, PA 19041). Using your time to explore jobs pays off in experience and learning about yourself, as well as the money or credit earned.

Stopouts have become so popular that up to half of the students at schools like Harvard, Swarthmore, and Stanford are stopping out for work experience. A Princeton junior took a job as a hospital orderly for ten months; he returned to school convinced that medicine was his vocation and that he wanted to be a doctor. Even though a medical orderly's job is very different from a doctor's, he learned about medicine as a *system,* about the different jobs within it, and became certain about the job he was after. Doug Patt, from Stanford University, has stopped out of college twice to see what the world of work was like. His second stopout included a job in a management agency for recording artists, where he learned about the music business on his own. He also toured with a blues singer. When he returned to college, he had a practical sense about the career he had chosen: film production. What does he say he learned? "I learned that if you want something in business, you've got to go for it."

Work experience, just like sports experience, club experience, family life, and classroom experience, counts as an educational pathway in your career development.

Consider Making a Career Change

It used to be that a young man would go into accounting and stay there. Or a man would become a successful salesperson, perhaps switch companies, but never dream of leaving sales. A student would choose medical school and then would practice medicine until retirement or death. Nowadays, the accountant may change to a computer career, the salesperson may open his own business, and the physician may change to a health management career. Today, a new group has entered the job market. It is not just comprised of graduating students, or the 8 million unemployed, or the 2 million homemakers each year who are looking for a job. For the first time in the United States, many job hunters are fully employed adults in career transition. Career changes in midlife are a new American phenomenon. The National Institute of Education reports that each year 40 million adults, or *36 percent of our working population,* are in career transition! Most of those who change careers are between 30 and 59 years old, with the average being 38 years old. They cite financial need as the primary motivation to career change. Reasons other than financial for so many changes are: overcrowded career fields, early retirement, women entering the work force from home, attained career goals, failure to be promoted, and no possibility for growth on the present job.

If you are in the market for a new career, the principles of going after what you want are the same whether you are a student, a full-time parent, or a full-time employed worker. You need to know what you have—personal assessment; what your options are—researching the job market; and how you can get what you want—job-hunting strategies that include how to locate the person who can hire you, write a résumé, interview successfully, and negotiate salary and promotion. Your personal assessment should include:

- Identify my transferable skills (problem-solving, budgeting, analyzing)
- Identify my content skills (engineering, home management, computer programming)
- Identify my interest areas (paid and nonpaid activities, hobbies, sports, clubs)
- Clarify my lifestyle values (friendships, family, children)
- Define my ideal job in terms of my skills, interests, values, and purpose in life
- Relate my skills, interests, and values to jobs

To begin your research of the job market, read the job descriptions in this book. If one job interests you, look at similar jobs in the same career cluster. Next, follow through your search by reading the trade journals and writing to the professional associations cited for each career. Translate what you learn about a career to your local level, or to the geographic part of the country where you want to live. Finally, remember that any changes in life tend to "rock the boat." Handling change is easier with the support of friends. Reaching out to your friends as you plan a career change will help smooth the transition.

Career change is one more way to look at your career development. As soon as you make a career choice, chances are that a change is going to follow. Plan for those changes. Think about what you are learning now; that will keep your change options open later.

Keep Your Options Open

Four-year college students can put off specific or specialized career decisions longer than two-year community college or technology students can. If you are a four-year student, or if you are taking time out from school or a job, or if you are changing jobs, take advantage of this extra time and explore your options as best you can. Keep in mind that all the technological and economic changes you've heard about in the job market in the past five years are still going on. All the changes in you that you've noticed are still going on, too. In other words, in the next few years, it can be a whole new ball game. If you stick with assessing your own skills, getting in tune with your values and interests as they change in your family place or workplace, and if you keep your career options open for new choices and changes, you can't go wrong.

ART, ARCHITECTURE, AND DESIGN

PERFORMING ARTS

Actor
Dancer
Musician

ARCHITECTURE

Architect
Landscape Architect

DESIGN

Commercial Artist
Industrial Designer
Interior Designer
Photographer

About these careers *Creativity and the ability to communicate, along with luck and drive, are necessary to succeed in the arts and design careers. This cluster of careers represents 887,200 jobs. That is about 0.9 million out of a total national work force of 102.1 million workers.*

Even in good times, the number of performing artists always exceeds the number of job openings. The difficulty of earning a living as a performer is one reason why many artists earn their living through teaching or routine jobs, such as waiting on tables and word-processing, that will support them while they continue to study and audition for performing-arts work.

Evening work is a regular part of the performing artist's life. Rehearsals may be held late at night and on weekends and holidays. When performances are given on the road, weekend traveling is often necessary. Besides the traveling required in the performing arts, many artists have to take any casual work they can find when a show closes and while waiting for another job. Travel, irregular hours, and unemployment are all very hard on family and social life.

A college degree counts less in the performing arts than in any other career. More important to artists are the professional schools of acting, dance, and music, which are located in the major cities where the work opportunities also exist. A professional school whose goal is to turn out the best musician, or actor, or dancer is the best place for your training. In order to find a professional school, write to the professional association at the end of the particular career description that interests you and ask for a list of approved schools.

Architects and designers spend long hours at the drawing board in well-equipped offices. New graduates usually begin as junior drafters in architectural firms, where they are closely supervised. Junior members of a firm are often asked to work overtime to meet a deadline and to do routine and tedious work that no one likes to do, until they gain experience and have paid their "professional beginner's dues."

Architect and landscape-architect education require a four-year or five-year program. Commercial art, interior design, and photography require a two-year or three-year professional or specialty school. Write to the professional association in the design career that interests you for a list of approved schools and colleges.

ACTOR

Entertains people through his interpretations of dramatic roles on the stage and in film.

What's It Like to Be an Actor?

Porter Anderson is a 23-year-old graduate student in theater arts at Ohio State University who was just accepted into the Asolo State Theater Company in Sarasota, Florida. He tells what the day is like for an actor/dancer in summer stock: "Dance warmup and cleaning up problems from the previous night's show begins the day from 9 a.m. to 12 noon. Then the actors eat a light lunch together, usually for an hour. From 1 p.m. to 5 p.m., we have a dance workout and rehearsal for a dance troupe, separate from our theater production, given periodically throughout the summer. The full company is called at 7 p.m., dance warmup is at 8:15 p.m., and the show begins at 8:45 p.m. Actors always eat dinner after the show. Then we go to bed around 2:00 a.m. The people who stay in acting are the ones who are driven by it and who feel they couldn't be happy in anything else." Anderson sees many young people wasting years of their lives because they can't see that they don't have the necessary talent, discipline, and determination to persevere in full professional work. What he likes best is the chance to express himself through characters in plays and the self-insight from playing different roles. He also likes the applause and the comraderie of actors. But, Anderson finds many things about being an actor very frustrating—the lack of money, the possibility of few "big breaks," not knowing where the next job will come from or when, losing a good acting job because you are an inch too tall or too short, and constantly having to lay yourself on the line for auditions. "However," concludes Anderson, "if the drive and the love for the art is there, all of the work seems worth the trouble. It is simply the only thing to do."

What Education and Skills Will I Need?

High school: College preparatory courses and as much acting as possible.

College: A theater arts or dramatics major offers experience in local productions as well as in summer stock. Acting experience is more important than the number of years you spend in college. Acting experience in your community can be the best way to become recognized as you build your acting record for future recommendations.

Personal skills: Dramatic skills, the patience and commitment to wait for work, and physical stamina for work under lights and for long rehearsals are needed to be an actor.

How Many Actors Are There and Where Do They Work?

There are 21,000 actors and actresses working in stage plays, films (including TV films), industrial shows, and commercials. In the winter, most of the employment opportunities on stage are in New York City. In the summer, many stock companies employ actors in the suburbs and resort areas. Motion pictures and films for television are made in Hollywood, although there are a few studios in New York, Miami, and Chicago. The main networks for television and radio are in New York and Los Angeles. Local television, cable, and radio stations also employ actors.

$ $ $ $ $

All professional actors belong to unions. In 1980, the minimum salary for a Broadway actor was $475 a week. Off-Broadway paid from $153 to $317 a week. Motion pictures offer a minimum of $259 a day to actors and $68 a day to extras. Most actors get little if any unemployment insurance, since they seldom have enough employment in any state to meet the eligibility requirements. The Actors Equity Association surveyed their 26,000 members and found 22,000 of them earned less than $5,000 a year!

What Is the Job Future?

Earning a living as an actor is often nearly impossible and almost always difficult. New York City is flooded with young, talented well-trained people looking desperately for the few jobs available. Even though more residential theaters are being organized, and more local television stations are beginning, the increasing number of young people entering acting each year offsets the new opportunities. Dinner theaters provide the fastest growing job openings in the country for actors. Public broadcasting systems and cable television are other good work possibilities for actors.

ACTOR

RELATED CAREERS

disc jockey
comedian
director
narrator
clown
radio announcer
television announcer

WHERE CAN I GET MORE INFORMATION?

Professional groups

American Theater Association
1000 Vermont Avenue, NW
Washington, D.C. 20005

The American National Theater and Academy (ANTA)
245 West 52 Street
New York, NY 10019

League of Professional Theater Training Programs
1860 Broadway, Suite 1515
New York, NY 10023

ANTA is an organization for actors looking for a placement service in New York City, for advice on how to select an agent, and for a list of producers. It is a good place to begin to learn about the job system in the theater.

Trade journal

Variety
154 West 46 Street
New York, NY 10036

DANCER

Expresses ideas and emotions through his body movements.

What's It Like to Be a Dancer?

Most dancers work together as a chorus in dance productions for the stage, movies, and television. Some are selected for special dance numbers, and a very few top artists do solo work. The few dancers who become choreographers create new ballets or dance routines. Others become dance directors who train dancers in new productions. Teachers usually teach in a professional dancing school or teach dance courses in colleges and universities.

Stephen Wynne, a 19-year-old scholarship dancer in the American Ballet Theater of New York City, says, "Seek out a reputable dance school, one associated with a company. Or ask a professional ballet dancer to recommend a good school. Get several opinions. Take as many classes as you can, as soon as you can, to get in shape. And most importantly—don't wait! If you aren't sure you want to be a dancer, you *will* be after a week or so in ballet school. Wynne discusses what he likes and doesn't like about being a dancer. "The only part of being a ballet dancer that I don't like is the dieting. I don't like to diet. Some dancers don't have to, but diet or no diet, we must all stay away from junk foods. The best part of dancing is the noticeable improvement—being able to do things today you couldn't do the day before. I like the excitement of controlling movement and the viewer's appreciation. I also love the discipline that dancing demands. In other words, the best thing about dance is dancing!"

What Education and Skills Will I Need?

Performers begin their training by the age of twelve or younger for commercial shows, and by the age of seven for ballet. Professional training includes 10 to 12 lessons a week for 11 to 12 months a year and many hours of practice. By 17 or 18 years of age, the dancer is prepared for audition. A good professional school is very important for the training it offers and for the connections it has for employment. In addition to dancing, dancers study music, literature, and history. A natural aptitude for dancing and a creative ability to express oneself through dance are necessary, along with the stability to face auditions and unstable working opportunities. An alternative to professional school training is a high school program leading to a dance major in college, sometimes within the physical education or theater arts department. This option can lead to performing or to teaching. Professional schools require teachers to be experienced performers. A dancer must have agility, coordination, grace, a sense of rhythm, a feeling for music, self-discipline, patience, good body build, physical stamina, and the ability to work with others as a team.

How Many Dancers Are There and Where Do They Work?

Seven thousand of the 23,000 dancers and dancing teachers are performers on stage, screen, and television. Eighty-five percent of all dancers are women, but in ballet and modern dance, half of the dancers are men. Performers work primarily in New York City, although there are now major dance companies in Los Angeles, San Francisco, Houston, Cincinnati, Miami, Chicago, Hartford, Seattle, Boston, and Philadelphia. Rarely can dancers perform after 30 to 35 years of age.

$ $ $ $ $

Performers belong to a union that sets the contracts and salaries. In 1980, ballet and stage productions started dancers at an average of $500 a week. Dance teachers with a master's degree in a college receive the same salary as other instructors, usually starting at $15,000 a year. See *College Professor.*

What Is the Job Future?

Very competitive. The supply of qualified and good dancers far exceeds employment opportunities. There are very few stage productions. Television and films will hire dancers for the few jobs open.

RELATED CAREERS

dance therapist	choreographer
dance teacher	dance critic
acrobat	

WHERE CAN I GET MORE INFORMATION?

Professional groups

American Guild of Musical Artists
1841 Broadway
New York, NY 10023

Ballet Society
New York State Theater
1865 Broadway
New York, NY 10023

Trade journal
Dance News
119 West 57 Street
New York, NY 10019

MUSICIAN

Expresses ideas and emotions through the music he plays.

What's It Like to Be a Musician?

Popular professional musicians play in concerts, dance bands in nightclubs, restaurants, and at special parties. The best known bands, rock groups, jazz groups, and solo performers often give concerts and perform on television. Classical musicians play in symphonic, opera, and theater orchestras, and in chamber groups. Almost all musicians do some teaching in order to earn a living. Music instructors usually teach vocal and instrumental music, classroom music appreciation, and individual lessons to students. Large churches hire full-time music directors and organists. Smaller churches employ school music teachers or local people on a part-time basis. Composer Paul Steg, professor of music at Northern Illinois University, finds that teaching during the academic year and attending student concerts every night leaves him no time for his first love in music—composing. He plans his summers away from the school setting, where he can put in the necessary hours and concentration to achieve the completed compositions he thinks about all winter. Dr. Steg has published a great variety of pieces, from viola solos for chamber music to junior high school band pieces.

What Education and Skills Will I Need?

Professional musicians usually begin their training at an early age in elementary school with intensive study in private lessons. Singers start voice training after they mature, and frequently study piano and dance, too. They audition for symphony orchestras, chamber and opera groups, and other professional music groups whenever they are ready. High school and college music teachers usually major in music in college, meeting particular certification needs according to the state in which they teach. There are over 400 music conservatories and schools that provide training in musical performance, history and theory.

How Many Musicians Are There and Where Do They Work?

There are 127,000 performing musicians, mostly working in New York, Nashville, Miami, Las Vegas, Chicago, Los Angeles, and New Orleans. Performing musicians are usually men. The classical jobs are with the 28 major symphonies, 88 metropolitan orchestras, and 1,100 community orchestras, dance bands, and rock groups.

$ $ $ $ $

Musicians belong to the American Federation of Musicians (AFL-CIO), and concert soloists belong to the American Guild of Musical Artists. In 1980, major symphony orchestra musicians earned from $350 to $600 a week. Teachers receive the same as other teachers in their school systems. Groups and singers get paid according to their reputation. Full-time church musicians average from $11,000 to $15,000 a year.

What Is the Job Future?

All music jobs are extremely competitive. There are many more talented musicians of all kinds—classical, pop, teachers, and performers—than jobs.

RELATED CAREERS

arranger	music therapist
composer	music salesperson
copyist	radio producer
music teacher	TV music producer

WHERE CAN I GET MORE INFORMATION?

Professional groups
American Federation of Musicians
1500 Broadway
New York, NY 10036

Music Educators National Conference
1902 Association Drive
Reston, VA 22091

Trade journals
Billboard
One Astor Plaza
1515 Broadway
New York, NY 10036

Rolling Stone
745 Fifth Avenue
New York, NY 10022

ARCHITECT

Plans and designs buildings and other structures.

What's It Like to Be an Architect?

An architect meets and discusses with his client the purpose, costs, preferences for style, and plan of the structure to be built. He considers the local building and zoning laws and makes the preliminary drawing of the building to show the client. The final design is a working one, including details of the plumbing, electrical, and heating systems. The architect helps his client select a building contractor and continues to represent the client until the structure is completed and all tests are made. Self-employed architects work on a variety of products, from homes, churches, and office buildings, to renewal projects, college campuses, new towns, and urban planning. When working for large architectural firms, architects often specialize in one phase of the work, such as design or construction contracts. This often requires working with engineers, city planners, and landscape architects.

What Education and Skills Will I Need?

High school: Preparation for college, with an emphasis on mathematics, physics, and art.

College: There are 87 accredited schools of architecture offering a five-year bachelor of architecture degree or a six-year

ARCHITECT

master of architecture degree. After three years of experience, an architect takes a state examination for a license to practice.

Personal skills: Capacity to solve technical problems and work independently, artistic skills, computer skills, and good business ability are necessary for architects. Architectural educators point out that energy conservation will require a stronger integration of engineering and computer skills to be a successful architect.

How Many Architects Are There and Where Do They Work?

There are 79,500 licensed architects. Forty percent of the architects are self-employed, and most of the others work for architectural firms. The majority of architects are employed in seven cities: Boston, Chicago, Los Angeles, New York, Philadelphia, San Francisco, and Washington. In addition, Houston, Dallas, and Phoenix are attracting new businesses and architects. The number of architects employed by corporations has increased. There are special problems with corporate employment, such as the need for a contract, the lack of liability insurance, and the need to deal with architectural registration boards who are only used to license private-practice architects.

$ $ $ $ $

In 1981, the average salary for all architects in the federal government was $32,000 a year. Architects starting their own practice often have more expenses than income in the first few years. Experienced architects in private practice often average $40,000 a year.

What Is the Job Future?

Jobs will be competitive through the 1980s because graduates outnumber the jobs.

RELATED CAREERS

civil engineer
urban planner
industrial designer
building contractor
landscape architect

WHERE CAN I GET MORE INFORMATION?

Professional group
The American Institute of Architects
1735 New York Avenue, NW
Washington, D.C. 20036

Trade journal
Architectural Record
McGraw-Hill Publications Company
Box 430
Hightstown, NJ 08520

LANDSCAPE ARCHITECT

Combines design with nature to design private yards, public parks, and commercial areas.

What's It Like to Be a Landscape Architect?

Landscape architects help plan projects with real-estate firms, or with cities planning an airport, or mall, or renewal program. Working with architects, engineers, and city planners, they plan and arrange trees, shrubbery, walk ways, and open spaces. After they get an approved plan, they prepare working drawings that show all details of buildings, roads, grading, and drainage structures in the planted areas. Then they invite landscape constructors to bid for the work. Phil Pryor, a graduate from Cornell, is the youngest member of a Boston firm, and so most of his time is spent drafting the plans of others. He looks forward to more designing and less drafting. "Most students don't know what landscape architecture is like and think it is something else. There are many transfers in the college program from other majors." Pryor advises students to visit and talk with landscape architects before they major in it.

What Education and Skills Will I Need?

High school: Preparation for college, with biology, botany, art, mathematics, and mechanical drawing.

College: Take a four-year or five-year college program in landscape architecture in one of the 28 approved colleges.

Personal skills: Landscape architects need talent in art and design, an interest in nature, and the ability to think creatively to express their thoughts with detail and precision.

How Many Landscape Architects Are There and Where Do They Work?

There are 15,000 landscape architects, and most are self-employed or work for architectural or engineering firms. Government agencies employ 40 percent of all landscape architects.

$ $ $ $ $

In 1980, landscape architects began at $13,500 to $18,000 a year. In 1981, those with the federal government started at $15,900 to $19,700 a year. Average salaries with experience were from $24,700 to $35,000 a year.

What Is the Job Future?

Jobs are expected to be very good through the 1980s. The increased demand results from the growing interest in city and regional environmental planning.

RELATED CAREERS

architect
environmental planner
community planner

WHERE CAN I GET MORE INFORMATION?

Professional group
American Society of Landscape Architects
1773 Connecticut Avenue, NW
Washington, D.C. 20009

Trade journal
Landscape Architect
Society of Landscape Architects
1500 Bardstown Road
Louisville, KY 40205

COMMERCIAL ARTIST

Creates the artwork for publications, films, textiles, greeting cards, and industrial products.

What's It Like to Be a Commercial Artist?

Albert Brochu, staff artist for a sports magazine, says, "It's tough to get the work you want right away, but take any commercial art job—all the experience you can get will lead to new jobs." Brochu was a freelance artist for three years, then he decided the work was too irregular for someone about to become a parent. The majority of commercial artists work with a team of artists under the supervision of an art director. The advertising artist creates the concept and artwork for promotional ideas to be coordinated in mass media. On the team are layout artists, who work up the arrangement of a rough visual sketch for a design; the renderers, who make a pastel or wash drawing; letterers, who add the writing to the ad; illustrators, who sketch a finer form of the design; and paste-up and mechanicals workers, who cut and paste the basic parts together using a ruling pen and drafting tools. In a small office, many of these jobs are done by the same person. Other commercial artists specialize in fashion illustrations, greeting cards, book illustrations, package design, textile design, painting, and industrial design. Peter A. Miller, Vermont portrait painter, took a job outside of the field of art when he finished college. He tells how at 28 he woke up one morning and asked himself, "What am I going to be when I grow up? If I had just a short time to live, what would I do with my life?" Miller calls this the "death-kid syndrome" and knows a lot of young men who experience it near the age of thirty. He decided he wanted to paint portraits more than anything else. He quit his job, got divorced, bought a few well-placed ads in local and regional publications, and turned his life around. He now makes about 40 percent of his living at painting and the other 60 percent from his job in marketing and selling handcrafted toys. The variety and change in working alone at his own art and working with others in business is just what he was after, at least for now.

COMMERCIAL ARTIST

What Education and Skills Will I Need?

High school: Preparation for an art school or a fine arts major in college. Art schools require an art aptitude test and an example of your work. Get as much art training and experience as possible.

College: A two-year art school or four-year college art program will prepare you for the better commercial jobs. As in all the arts, demonstration of your ability and talent is more important than a degree.

Personal skills: Artistic ability, imagination, a distinctive style, and the capacity to translate ideas onto paper are necessary in commercial art.

How Many Artists Are There and Where Do They Work?

About 120,000 people work as commercial and graphic artists and designers. They are employed in the major cities of New York, Chicago, Los Angeles, Boston, and Washington, but some are employed in every city. The majority are staff artists working for advertising agencies, commercial art studios, and advertising departments of stores and companies. A considerable number of freelance commercial artists work part-time in order to spend the rest of their time on fine arts.

$ $ $ $ $

Artists in entry-level paste-up or layout jobs often make as little as minimum wage. Art directors, designers, and well-known freelance illustrators earn from $30,000 to $40,000 a year and more.

What Is the Job Future?

Chances for work and promotions will continue to be very competitive through the 1980s. Some jobs are needed more than others, and freelance artists, paste-up artists, and mechanical artists will find work.

RELATED CAREERS

industrial designer
interior designer
set designer
fashion designer

WHERE CAN I GET MORE INFORMATION?

Professional groups
The Graphic Artists Guild
30 East 20 Street, Room 405
New York, NY 10003

National Art Education Association
1916 Association Drive
Reston, VA 22091

Trade journal
Illustrator Magazine
500 South Fourth Street
Minneapolis, MN 55415

INDUSTRIAL DESIGNER

Designs or arranges objects and materials to best show off a product's appearance, function, and value.

What's It Like to Be an Industrial Designer?

Industrial designers study their company's product and competing products to decide possibilities for change. They sketch the product, then make a model of it, often in clay. After company engineers, sales and market research personnel, and production supervisors are consulted, the model is approved and produced. Ray Ingaus, an industrial designer for General Electric, likes his work because he says it is challenging to do and always a chance to learn something new. "It is interesting because I can watch my designs being fabricated in our own tool room. Also, being an industrial designer, I am constantly involved with production, which gives me a chance to spend a large part of my time on the production floor as a troubleshooter on old fixtures as well as new designs."

What Education and Skills Will I Need?

High school: Preparation for college, with courses in art, drafting, and mathematics.

College: Take one of the 33 college programs approved by the Industrial Designers Society of America for industrial design.

Personal skills: Creativity, artistic and drawing skills, ability to see familiar objects in new ways, ability to work with people who are not designers, and an interest in business and sales are needed for success.

How Many Industrial Designers Are There and Where Do They Work?

Of the 13,000 industrial designers, 9,000 are men. Most work for large manufacturing companies or for design consulting firms in New York, Chicago, Los Angeles, and San Francisco.

$ $ $ $ $

In 1980, beginners started at $15,000 a year. Designers with two years experience averaged $18,000 a year.

What Is the Job Future?

Jobs will be competitive for college graduates of industrial design. The markets for new products are low when the economy is in recession.

RELATED CAREERS

architect
fashion designer
commercial artist

WHERE CAN I GET MORE INFORMATION?

Professional group
Industrial Designers Society of America
1717 N Street, NW
Washington, D.C. 20036

Trade journal
Industrial Design
717 Fifth Avenue
New York, NY 10022

INTERIOR DESIGNER

Plans and supervises the design and arrangement of building interiors and furnishings.

What's It Like to Be an Interior Designer?

Boston designer Michael S. Abdou, a member of the American Society of Interior Design, says: "Your work is never duplicated—every day and every client is different. A designer is a guide who helps home owners get the styles and colors they want. Making the color schemes after you work with a client takes most of the time." Abdou is well-established in his own firm, and he always takes the summers off because clients usually are not in their city homes in the summer. He advises young men who like to create things "to go to the best school of art or design you can get into."

What Education and Skills Will I Need?

High school: Preparation for art school or a degree in fine arts.

College: Go to a three-year art school or institute of interior design, or take a degree in architecture. A college degree or a three-year professional school degree is required to be a professional member of the American Society of Interior Design, which is necessary for the best jobs.

Personal skills: Artistic talent, color sense, good taste, imagination, good business judgment, and the ability to work with detail are needed to be a successful designer.

How Many Interior Designers Are There and Where Do They Work?

Half of the 35,000 full-time interior designers are men. The majority work in large cities. Some have their own firms. Others work for design firms, large department and furniture stores, hotel and restaurant chains, architects, and home furnishing magazines.

$ $ $ $ $

In 1980, many art school graduates began at $8,000 to $14,000 a year. Experienced decorators with a reputation in their area earn from $15,000 to $25,000 a year, while highly successful designers earn over $50,000 a year. In addition to salary, many designers earn a commission based on their sale of rugs, draperies, furniture, and materials used in their design.

What Is the Job Future?

Talented art school or college graduates with good business ability will get the few jobs through the 1980s. Like most creative work, interior design is very competitive, as many young people flock to the city for the small number of jobs.

RELATED CAREERS

exhibit designer
display worker
fabric designer

WHERE CAN I GET MORE INFORMATION?

Professional group
American Society of Interior Designers
730 Fifth Avenue
New York, NY 10019

Trade journal
Interiors
130 East 59 Street
New York, NY 10022

PHOTOGRAPHER

Takes pictures as an artistic or technical occupation, such as portrait photography, commercial photography, and photojournalism.

What's It Like to Be a Photographer?

As a writer uses words, a photographer uses his camera to portray people, places, and events. Some specialize in scientific, medical, or engineering photography, and their pictures enable thousands of people to see a world normally hidden from view. Others specialize in portraits, commercial photography, industrial work, or photojournalism. Photojournalism combines photographic ability with newspaper work. Most photographers own several different cameras depending on their specialty. John Nelson has been in partnership in a portrait business with his wife, Rosanna, for thirty years in a small city. They have two galleries in neighboring suburbs and are successful because they work long hours and have always been careful in their work. Nelson wants people to know that "if you're going into the photography business, you will need to know about business management, and how to relax people and promote your business as much as how to use the camera. Photography has come of age in the last fifteen years, with technology and materials enabling more creative work. With the tools available, there's no limitation on creativity."

What Education and Skills Will I Need?

Education varies from on-the-job learning to courses leading to a degree in photography. The future belongs to the photographer whose training and experience enable him to do more than other photographers can do. Preparation for a career in photography must include knowledge of the field in which photography will be applied. Economics, geography, international affairs, and journalism are important for the photojournalist. A career in advertising photography requires knowledge of art and design and some background in advertising.

Personal skills: Photographers need good eyesight, artistic ability, and manual dexterity. News photographers need the ability to see a potential good photo and act quickly; portrait photographers need the ability to help people relax. Original ideas are necessary for success in freelance work.

How Many Photographers Are There and Where Do They Work?

There are 91,000 photographers and half of them are in the portrait and commercial-art-studio businesses. Salaried photographers work for the government, television broadcasting, newspapers and magazines, private industry, and advertising agencies. Over forty percent of all photographers are self-employed.

$ $ $ $ $

In 1981, beginners earned from $250 to $335 a week. The average salary for newspaper photographers was $441 a week. Photographers in business for themselves and with a national reputation make much more than these figures. The top magazine photographers with a national reputation earn over $50,000 a year. Most, however, work very hard in an office in their home for salaries between $14,000 and $24,000 a year.

What Is the Job Future?

Portrait photography is a very competitive business. The newspaper, business and industry, law enforcement, and scientific fields are expected to need more photographers through the 1980s. The well-trained people with strong technical backgrounds will have the best opportunities.

RELATED CAREERS

commercial artist
illustrator
painter
sculptor

WHERE CAN I GET MORE INFORMATION?

Professional group
Professional Photographers of America, Inc.
1090 Executive Way
Des Plaines, IL 60018

Trade journal
Popular Photography
Davis Publishing
1 Park Avenue
New York, NY 10016

PHOTOGRAPHER

BUSINESS: ADMINISTRATION AND MANAGEMENT

Administrative Secretary
Business Executive
Funeral Director and Embalmer
Hotel, Motel, Restaurant Manager
Personnel and Labor Relations
Purchasing Agent
Retail Buyer

About these careers *There are 9.4 million managers and administrators in business and business-related jobs. Your chances for getting into a business-management training program in a major corporation are competitive, even with a college degree. A Master of Business Administration (MBA) is your best bet for the top management programs. People in business come from all college majors and backgrounds. Many are from liberal arts programs, with majors in economics, accounting, statistics, and law.*

For young men trying to advance in business, "Learn the business from top to bottom, establish a 'winner' reputation, and plan to spend long hours at work. Be prepared to spend 25 years getting to the top," warns the Chief Operating Officer of the Equity Life Assurance Society.

Owners and managers of small businesses, such as restaurants, lodgings, and funeral homes, usually work very long hours. They can be on call 24 hours a day 7 days a week because these are service businesses. Almost one out of five managers are self-employed. However, the number of self-employed managers is declining, and this trend is expected to continue through the 1980s.

The major department stores have formal training programs in merchandising for their management trainees. These programs usually last from 6 to 8 months and combine classroom instruction with store operations and policies, providing the fundamentals of merchandising and management. To be promoted to merchandise manager, most assistant buyers need 5 years of experience and exceptional ability. Many managers advance further into executive jobs in large retail stores or chains. Retail managers often work more than 40 hours a week because of sales conferences and travel.

Graduate study in industrial relations, economics, business, or law provides sound preparation for work and advancement in labor relations. Corporations are just beginning to get into the graduate education business. The 1980s will see more and more corporate educational institutes where you can learn the specific business management, engineering, selling, and investment skills you need for changing careers and advancement. You can get a master's degree at Arthur D. Little's graduate Management Education Institute in Cambridge, Massachusetts, or a master's degree in a computer specialty at the Wang Institute. Wang offers one of the few software engineering degrees in the world. Merrill Lynch, Pierce, Fenner & Smith has opened its own college for stockbrokers. McDonald's Hamburger University teaches management, personnel, finance, and taxation. Both IBM and the American Telephone and Telegraph Company spend millions of dollars to educate their full-time employees in skills needed on the job as well as in management skills for advancement. When you are planning advancement through education, be sure to check the company you work for, or want to work for, first. Take a lesson from the men who have successfully expected the companies they work for to train them at corporate expense.

ADMINISTRATIVE SECRETARY

Processes and transmits information to a staff and to people in other organizations; attends to business activities depending on the nature of the employer's business.

What's It Like to Be a Secretary?

The computer revolution is changing the role of secretary. Word processors, the computers with typewriterlike keyboards, are taking over the routine reports and other rote clerical chores. Their use has just begun. One million word processors have been installed in small and large offices, and another million and a half will be installed by 1983. Instead of spending 20 percent of his day typing, the typical secretary will spend only 10 percent in the years ahead. These word processors are expected to give secretaries more time and opportunity to perform administrative tasks now completed by managers. If this happens, some experts believe the serious shortage of secretaries may subside and the gap in wages between executive and secretaries may narrow somewhat. Men who want to use the secretarial entry level as a springboard to learn the business will find the word processor an advantage. Bernard Schwartz, Director of Communication of the International Information/Processing Association, says, "Word processing is a good field for career-minded men. Many of our 14,000 members started out as secretaries, and today some of them are earning as much as $50,000 a year, because word processing was a career path to management. In the 1980s, more secretaries will have such opportunities."

What Education and Skills Will I Need?

High school: Preparation for business college, secretarial school, community college, or four-year college.

College: Get one or two years of specialized training in the secretarial field of your choice, or take secretarial courses along with another major or in correspondence school. Computer science and word processing are a must for the better jobs that lead to management.

ADMINISTRATIVE SECRETARY

Personal skills: Secretaries must have an interest in detail and organization, and an ability to be accurate and to follow through on assigned work.

How Many Secretaries Are There and Where Do They Work?

There are 2.7 million people in occupations requiring secretarial or stenographic skills, and about 5 percent of them are men. Half of all secretaries work in public service organizations such as schools and hospitals. The other half work in banks, insurance companies, real estate firms, and other business and industrial companies.

$ $ $ $ $

Secretarial salaries vary with the location and the job. For example, in 1980, secretaries in the Northeast made an average of $13,364 a year; in the North Central area, $14,066 a year; in the West, $14,586 a year; and in the South, $12,818 a year. A general secretary made an average of $11,856 a year; a bilingual secretary, $12,844 a year; a legal secretary, $13,572 a year; and an administrative or executive secretary ranged from $13,416 a year to working for the top company executive at $19,812 a year.

What Is the Job Future?

The demand for qualified secretaries is expected to increase through the 1980s. Secretarial schools graduate only two-thirds of the secretaries needed to fill 305,000 openings each year. The rise in paperwork, especially in finance, real estate, and health, create a demand for more secretaries just as fewer people are entering the field.

RELATED CAREERS

bookkeeper
office manager
administrative assistant

WHERE CAN I GET MORE INFORMATION?

Professional groups

National Secretaries Association
2440 Pershing Road, Suite G–10
Kansas City, MO 64108

9 to 5
YWCA
140 Clarendon Street
Boston, MA 02116

BUSINESS EXECUTIVE

Directs or plans the work of others in order to run a business at a profit.

What's It Like to Be a Business Executive?

Business executives are managers who direct workers in sales, research, production, accounting, and purchasing. They often work in company teams to decide about sales, personnel, public relations, and how the work must be done. Directors of training programs hiring future executives for their corporations from among college graduates look for self-starters, those people who can use their initiative, who have an observing eye to see what needs to be done, who like responsibility, and who have high standards for fairness. They must have a thoroughness, not necessarily brilliance, and persistence to be good in their job.

What Education and Skills Will I Need?

High school: Preparation for college in whatever major that interests you, taking as broad a program as you can do well. Participate in extracurricular activities that teach management qualities of leadership and awareness. Athletics are especially important for you if you want competitive experiences.

College: Many executive training programs recruit from

liberal arts students. The ability to think and make decisions and an interest in the particular training program are special qualities that corporations look for. A Master of Business Administration is a good alternative to an executive training program right out of college. When Dr. Thomas J. First, Jr., President and Chief Executive Officer of Hospital Corporation of America, was asked where he trained in business management, he replied, "I have my 'MBA' from some of the best businessmen in the world." In other words, men in top positions often learned on-the-job, and their education came from the industry, not from graduate schools.

Personal skills: Decision-making skills, assertiveness, fairness, and an interest in business are important for executives.

How Many Business Executives Are There and Where Do They Work?

About 10 million salaried persons manage the nation's businesses and 2.5 million are college graduates. There are thousands more who are owners of their own businesses, although small business managers are expected to decline in the 1980s.

$ $ $ $ $

In 1980, college graduates entering management trainee programs received $15,000 to $21,000 a year. Middle-management salaries range from $25,000 to $50,000 in our major corporations. When you think about middle-management and top-management salaries, be aware that salaries are fast becoming only a small part of what is known as the "executive compensation package," or perks. For example, the executive with a salary of $50,000 a year gets an additional $70,000 in rewards. The executive with a $200,000 salary may earn as much as $580,000 more a year in bonuses, long-term incentives, fringe benefits, and perks.

What Is the Job Future?

In the 1970s, business managers were one of the growing occupations. Because of recession and inflation, thousands of managers have been laid off. The largest number of job openings are for people with Masters in Business Administration. The best opportunities are for management specialists in big business. Self-employed managers are decreasing in numbers as the trend moves toward supermarkets, chains, and merging business firms.

RELATED CAREERS

hospital administrator
hotel-motel manager
sales manager
marketing manager

WHERE CAN I GET MORE INFORMATION?

Professional group
The American Management Association
135 West 50 Street
New York, NY 10020

Trade journals
Business Management
22 West Putnam Avenue
Greenwich, CT 06830

Fortune
Time-Life Building
New York, NY 10020

MBA
MBA Enterprises
373 Fifth Avenue
New York, NY 10016

FUNERAL DIRECTOR AND EMBALMER

A director helps families with business arrangements necessary for the funeral service and burial; an embalmer prepares the deceased for viewing and burial.

What's It Like to Be a Funeral Director and Embalmer?

A funeral director arranges for the deceased to be moved to the funeral home, obtains the information needed for the death certificate, and discusses the details of the funeral with the family, such as the time and place of service, clergy and organist, selection of casket and clothing, and provision of burial or cremation. He also makes arrangements with the cemetery, and places obituary notices in the newspapers. The director attends to the floral displays; provides cars for the family, pallbearers, and ushers; sees guests to their seats; and may serve a family for months following the funeral until all social security and insurance claims are settled. Few occupations require the tact, discretion, and compassion called for in the work of a funeral director. Families of the deceased are under considerable emotional stress and are often bewildered by the many details of the occasion.

An embalmer replaces the deceased's blood with a preservative fluid, applies cosmetics to the body to give it a natural appearance, dresses the body, and places it in the casket selected by the family. Embalming is a sanitary and preservative measure required by law.

What Education and Skills Will I Need?

High school: Preparation for school of mortuary science, with high school courses in biology, chemistry, speech, and psychology. Work in a part-time or summer job in a local funeral home while in high school.

College: Half of the states require one year of college before the one-year training in mortuary science offered at 35 accredited schools. For the list of accredited schools write to:

American Board of Funeral Service Education, 201 Columbia Avenue, Fairmont, West Virginia 26554. A license is needed to practice embalming, and an apprenticeship of one or two years must be served; an examination is required by each state.

Personal skills: Composure, tact, ability to communicate easily with the public, and a desire to comfort people in sorrow.

How Many Funeral Directors Are There and Where Do They Work?

There are 45,000 licensed funeral directors and embalmers and 98 percent are men. Most funeral workers are employed in small family-owned businesses with two or three embalmers.

$ $ $ $ $

After one year of training, apprentices started from $150 to $250 a week in 1980. Directors and embalmers earned from $15,000 to $30,000 a year, and owners of the business earned more than $50,000.

What Is the Job Future?

The number of mortuary-school graduates has about equaled the number of jobs available. Good opportunities for jobs are expected through the 1980s. It is a well-paid career for only two years of post-high-school education.

RELATED CAREERS

small business manager
family business owner
minister

WHERE CAN I GET MORE INFORMATION?

Professional group
National Funeral Directors Association
135 West Wells Street
Milwaukee, WI 53203

Trade journal
The Director
135 West Wells Street
Milwaukee, WI 53203

HOTEL, MOTEL, CLUB, OR RESTAURANT MANAGER

Manages food and lodging establishments for a profitable business, providing maximum comfort for guests.

What's It Like to Be in a Food-Lodging Career?

Hotel managers decide about room rates and credit policy, direct the kitchen and dining rooms, and manage the housekeeping, accounting, and maintenance departments of hotels. They are also responsible for problems as they arise. The job depends on the size of the hotel. Large hotels and chains offer more specialization; a small hotel or self-employed owner often does all of the jobs, including front-desk clerical work, advertising, and personnel. Many opportunities for experienced restaurant managers can be found in club management. Every country club in the nation needs a manager, as do service clubs, private clubs, and athletic clubs. A country club in Wichita, Kansas, for instance, pays their manager $50,000 a year, plus a car and other benefits.

What Education and Skills Will I Need?

High school: Preparation for college or business college. Summer work in resorts, hotels, and restaurants helps gain experience and knowledge about what the job will be like. Major in hotel administration, or go to a community college, or take a correspondence course in hotel-motel management.

College: Large hotels with training programs look for graduates of hotel and restaurant administration. Small hotels and owner-manager lodges and restaurants do not require a degree, but do require interest, motivation, an original idea, and capital.

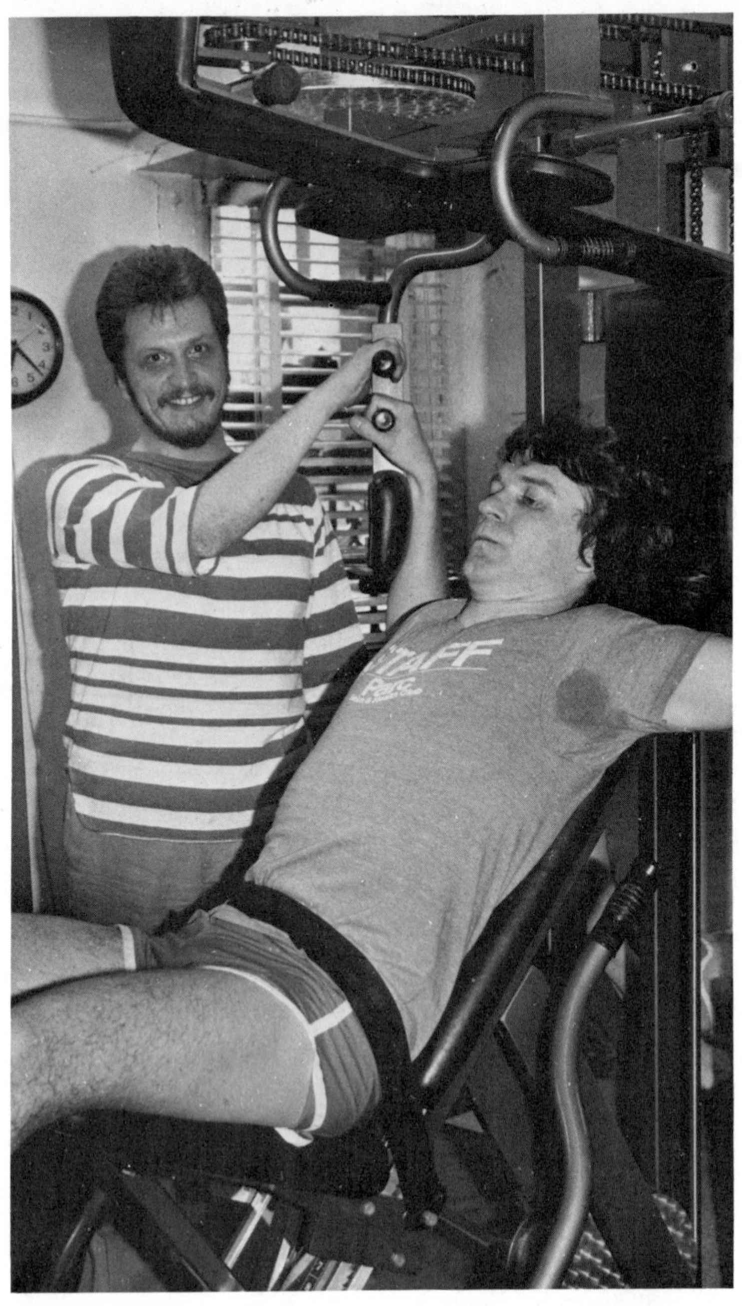

CLUB MANAGER

Personal skills: Initiative, self-discipline, and ability to organize and concentrate on detail are needed in food-lodging careers.

How Many Hotel-Motel-Restaurant Managers Are There and Where Do They Work?

There are 84,000 hotel and motel managers, and more than 40,000 of them are owner-managers. In addition, there are 707,000 restaurant and bar managers.

$ $ $ $ $

A beginning graduate from a hotel school starts at $13,500 in a training program in large hotels. In 1981, hotel managers ranged from $20,000 to $80,000 a year. Hotel food and beverage managers earned from $16,000 to $40,000 a year.

What Is the Job Future?

Chances for jobs for the college graduate who has specialized in hotel administration will be very good through the 1980s. Small lodges and restaurants in cities and resort areas are often started by young people, and even though the business is competitive, many original ideas have resulted in a living and a satisfying lifestyle for the owners.

RELATED CAREERS

apartment manager
office manager
sales manager

WHERE CAN I GET MORE INFORMATION?

Professional groups

American Hotel and Motel Association
888 Seventh Avenue
New York, NY 10019

Club Managers Association of America
7615 Winterberry Place
P.O. Box 34482
Washington, D.C. 20034

Council on Hotel, Restaurant, and Institutional Education
1522 K Street, NW
Washington, D.C. 20005

Trade journals
Hotel and Motel Management
Sun-Times Building, Room 534
401 North Wabash Avenue
Chicago, IL 60611

Nation's Restaurant News
2 Park Avenue
New York, NY 10016

PERSONNEL AND LABOR RELATIONS

Personnel workers try to hire and keep the best employees available for the success of a business or government. Labor relations workers handle union-management relations in unionized firms.

What's It Like to Be in Personnel and Labor Relations?

Personnel and labor relations represent management for the business or government agency, providing the link between management and employees. Personnel workers try to attract the best employees available and match them to the jobs they do best. Dealing with people is the essential activity of personnel workers. Some specialize in filling job vacancies by interviewing, selecting, and recommending applicants for job openings; some handle wage and salary administration; others specialize in training and career development on-the-job, and still others work in employee benefits.

Labor relations workers advise management on collective bargaining sessions and participation in contract negotiations with the union. They also handle labor relations matters that happen everyday. Arvid Anderson, Director of New York City's Office of Collective Bargaining, is the country's outstanding labor "referee." He studied labor economics at the University of Wisconsin in the 1940s and says that his success "flows from an insistence on being low-keyed, methodical, and totally committed to the concept of collective bargaining."

What Education and Skills Will I Need?

High school: Preparation for college, with emphasis on English and social studies.

College: Personnel and labor relations people come from a great variety of college majors. Some have been in business administration, psychology, sociology, or industrial relations. Most companies look for a college graduate with the personal characteristics they think would be good for the company. A law degree is becoming highly desirable for contract negotiations in labor relations.

Personal skills: Ability to speak and write effectively, work as a member of a team, see opposing viewpoints, and work with people of all different levels of education are necessary skills in personnel and labor relations.

How Many Personnel and Labor Relations Workers Are There and Where Do They Work?

There are 178,000 personnel and labor relations workers. Two-thirds of them work for private industry and others for government agencies.

$ $ $ $ $

In 1980, beginners started for private industry from $14,800 to $21,900 a year. Directors of personnel earned between $27,719 and $49,730 a year.

What Is the Job Future?

Opportunities in personnel jobs for the new graduate are very limited and competitive. Labor relations is even more difficult. The best chances will be for those with a master's degree in industrial relations or with a law degree.

WHERE CAN I GET MORE INFORMATION?

Professional group
American Society for Personnel Administration
30 Park Drive
Berea, OH 44017

Trade journal
The Personnel Administrator
30 Park Drive
Berea, OH 44017

PURCHASING AGENT

Negotiates and contracts to purchase equipment, supplies, and other merchandise for a firm.

What's It Like to Be a Purchasing Agent?

A purchasing agent, sometimes called an industrial buyer, is responsible for getting the best dollar value for supplies he has to buy for his firm. He buys raw materials, office supplies, furniture, and business machines. A purchasing agent checks on deliveries to be sure the work flow of the firm isn't interrupted for lack of materials. He works with other departments within his company, such as engineering and shipping, in order to coordinate the supplies with what is needed. Bruce Gragham, Purchasing Agent for General Electric, says that developing a good business relationship with suppliers is crucial for cost savings, favorable payment terms, and quick delivery on emergency orders. He builds his supplier market by comparing listings in catalogues and trade journals and those of telephone suppliers. Gragham meets often with salesworkers to look at their samples, and he attends demonstrations of equipment.

Often, he invites suppliers to bid on large orders and then selects the lowest bidder who can meet his firm's requirements for quality and delivery date. Gragham and his family are tennis players. He likes his job because "it's a good-paying 40-hour week, with plenty of time left for family and tennis."

What Education and Skills Will I Need?

High school: Preparation for college. Large firms hire college graduates for their training programs.

College: Many agents come from backgrounds in engineering, accounting, and economics. Understanding the computer and its uses is a necessity in a purchasing job.

Personal skills: Skill in analyzing numbers and technical data, ability to work and get along with others, and memory for detail are all necessary skills for a purchasing agent.

How Many Purchasing Agents Are There and Where Do They Work?

There are 172,000 purchasing agents and over half work in manufacturing firms. Others work for government agencies, hospitals, and schools.

$ $ $ $ $

In 1980, purchasing agents started at $12,000 to $14,000 a year, experienced agents earned $25,000 a year, and managers made over $50,000 a year.

What Is the Job Future?

Chances for jobs are very good, especially for the technically trained college graduates in electronics and communications and in industrial machinery. Two-year graduates will find good opportunities in small firms.

RELATED CAREERS

retail buyer
procurement services manager
wholesaler

WHERE CAN I GET MORE INFORMATION?

Professional group
National Association of Purchasing Management, Inc.
11 Park Place
New York, NY 10007

Trade journal
Purchasing
C-M Business Publications
205 East 42 Street
New York, NY 10017

RETAIL BUYER

Purchases merchandise for his firm to resell at a profit.

What's It Like to Be a Retail Buyer?

Merchandise managers divide the budget among retail buyers, decide how much merchandise to stock, and assign each buyer to purchase certain goods. Retail buyers work with their merchandise manager, manufacturers' representatives, store executives, salesworkers, and customers. Assisting with sales promotions is also part of their job. They work on a very busy schedule with a lot of hustle with all kinds of people. Irv Lief, a former New York City Macy's trainee, has just taken a new job in merchandising at Innes of Wichita, Kansas. He loves the fast pace of the work and doesn't think it matters whether you work for a large store or a small one. "Getting the goods to the customers at the right time for the best profit is exactly the daily challenge I like to live with. My wife is also in business," says Lief, "and we both like a career-oriented lifestyle."

What Education and Skills Will I Need?

High school: Preparation for business school, art school, a merchandising program, or a liberal arts degree.

College: Take a two-year or four-year course that includes business, marketing, fashion, merchandising, and art. Prepare for a department-store training program for buyers, such as the prestigious Bloomingdale's program.

Personal skills: Buyers must be able to work fast, be good planners, and be able to communicate with salesworkers, buyers, and sellers all at the same time.

How Many Retail Buyers Are There and Where Do They Work?

There are 150,000 buyers and merchandising managers. Half of them work for clothing and general department stores in major cities. Sixty percent of them are men.

$ $ $ $ $

In 1980, most buyers earned between $19,000 and $28,000 a year.

What Is the Job Future?

Jobs will be competitive through the 1980s, since it is a glamorous job and many college graduates go after it. Assertive, fast-working people who like to hustle are the ones that will get these jobs.

RELATED CAREERS

comparison shopper
merchandise manager
manufacturer's sales representative
wholesale trade sales representative

WHERE CAN I GET MORE INFORMATION?

Professional group
The Fashion Group, Inc.
9 Rockefeller Plaza
New York, NY 10020

Trade journals
Marketing Times
380 Lexington Avenue
New York, NY 10017

Women's Wear Daily
7 East 12 Street
New York, NY 10003

BUSINESS: ADVERTISING AND MARKETING

Advertising
Market Researcher
Public Relations

About these careers *There are 286,000, or about one-quarter of a million, jobs in advertising, public relations, and marketing. Many employers prefer college graduates who have liberal arts training with degrees in journalism or business. However, there is no correlation between a particular educational background and success in these fields.*

People in advertising work under great pressure. They are expected to produce quality ads in as short a time as possible. Sometimes, they must work long and irregular hours in order to make last-minute changes in ads and meet deadlines. Advertising can be a satisfying career for men and women who enjoy variety, excitement, creative challenges, and competition. Unlike people in many other careers, advertising workers experience the satisfaction of having their work in print, on television, or on radio, even though they themselves remain unknown to the public.

Market-research people usually work in modern, centrally located offices. Some PR and market researchers, especially those employed by independent firms, do a considerable amount of traveling. As assistants and junior analysts in market research gain experience, they may assume responsibility for specific market-research projects, or advance to supervisory positions. Outstanding workers become market-research directors or vice presidents in marketing and sales.

Advancement is very competitive in advertising, public relations, and marketing. Advertising is a glamorous and popular career, with many highly qualified people seeking jobs. In advertising, copywriters and account executives may advance to more responsible work in their specialties, or to managerial jobs. Some exceptional public relations, or "PR," people become partners or establish their own agencies.

ADVERTISING

Persuades people to buy the firm's products or use the firm's services.

What's It Like to Be in Advertising?

Madison Avenue advertising in New York City is one of the most glamorous careers in the country. It is a creative and imaginative job where the salaries can be the highest. The commodity is the person's talent and the person must produce the idea, the copy, and the business that will maintain the client's product. The career of advertising includes a number of different positions: *Advertising managers,* who are responsible for planning budget and for overall supervision; *creative workers* such as *writers, artists,* and *designers,* who develop and produce advertisements; and *business* and *sales workers,* who handle the arrangements for broadcasting the ads on radio and TV, for publishing them in newspapers or magazines, or for mailing them directly to the public.

What Education and Skills Will I Need?

High school: College preparatory program, with as much work in language as possible. Writing must be learned exceptionally well. Working on school publications, learning to be a good observer, noticing how people respond, and selling are experiences that will be helpful in advertising.

College: Most advertising agencies prefer a liberal arts student with a major in advertising, marketing, journalism, or business. Community college, business college, and art programs can get you a start in advertising. The most common way to enter the field of advertising without a degree is to begin in a department store advertising program.

Personal skills: Imagination, creativity, and a flair for language and selling are required for success in advertising.

How Many Advertising Workers Are There and Where Do They Work?

Almost half of the 170,000 people in advertising work in New York and Chicago. About 100,000 of them work in advertising agencies. The rest work for manufacturers, retail stores, broadcasting stations, and publishers.

ADVERTISING

$ $ $ $ $

The top beginning salaries are paid to outstanding liberal arts graduates, usually men. In 1980, they started from $10,000 to $18,000 a year. Those with an MBA often started at $25,000 a year. Salaries vary according to the size of the agency. An account executive in a large New York City agency often makes $40,000 a year, and a few make much more.

What Is the Job Future?

Competition in advertising is very stiff for everyone, although a moderate increase in number of jobs is expected through the 1980s. Like other glamour jobs, advertising attracts many creative young people every year.

RELATED CAREERS

public relations
fundraiser
lobbyist
promotion manager

WHERE CAN I GET MORE INFORMATION?

Professional groups

American Advertising Federation
1225 Connecticut Avenue, NW
Washington, D.C. 20036

American Association of Advertising Agencies
666 Third Avenue
New York, NY 10017

Trade journal

Advertising Age
J. J. Graham
740 North Rush Street
Chicago, IL 60611

MARKET RESEARCHER

Plans, implements, and analyzes surveys to learn more about people's wants and needs.

What's It Like to Be a Market Researcher?

"Finding out how much money people spend on what products and which services is a fascinating career for anyone interested in why people do things," says Don Levine about his job in Chicago. He takes public opinion surveys, studies and analyzes the sales of the company he works for and of competitive companies. Levine looks at the population changes, income levels, and consumer credit policies, and reports to his company management. Management uses this kind of information to decide brand names, packaging, and designs for their products; new locations for the company; and types of advertising their products need. Married with two young children, Levine says he is almost never home because "getting a good start in this business means putting in long hours during the first five years."

What Education and Skills Will I Need?

High school: Preparation for college, with emphasis on English and mathematics.

College: Attend business, community, or four-year college. Researchers come from business administration, economics, sociology, psychology, and liberal arts programs with a variety of majors. Computer science skills are a basic requirement.

Personal skills: Market researchers should be resourceful in analyzing data, and should be able to write clearly.

How Many Market Researchers Are There and Where Do They Work?

There are 29,000 full-time market researchers. The majority of market researchers are employed by manufacturing companies, advertising agencies, and market research firms in New York and Chicago. Others work in department stores, for radio and television stations, and in university and government research centers all over the country.

$ $ $ $ $

In 1980, college graduates started from $12,000 to $17,000 a year. Experienced market researchers such as senior analysts made over $27,000 a year. Directors who had more than fifteen years' experience averaged $50,000 a year.

What Is the Job Future?

Chances for work will be good through the 1980s. Opportunities will be available for persons with skills in statistics and computer science. The growth in health care facilities, banks, and accounting firms will result in more marketing jobs.

RELATED CAREERS

economist
political scientist
urban planner
social welfare research worker

WHERE CAN I GET MORE INFORMATION?

Professional group
American Marketing Association
250 Wacker Street
Chicago, IL 60606

Trade journal
Marketing News
222 South Riverside Plaza
Chicago, IL 60606

PUBLIC RELATIONS

Develops and distributes persuasive materials in order to create a favorable public reputation.

What's It Like to Be in Public Relations?

Public relations (PR) people plan publicity that they think will be most effective, communicate with the people who would use the publicity, write press releases for newspapers and magazines, and write brochures and pamphlets about a company or product. They arrange special speaking engagements for company officials and often write speeches. They work with films, slides, video, and all types of audio-visual equipment. Their work is often under tension and pressure caused by deadlines and last-minute newspaper releases. Public relations workers must be knowledgeable about all media and decide what is the most effective way to put across their ideas. Michael Wolfe, a Cincinnati PR man just starting his own firm, has had four years of experience in Chicago. He says he now works twice as hard and at much more risk, but he thinks he is where he wants to be—using every idea he ever had. "My long hours seem to be easier on the family, now that the business is my own. Besides that, they wanted to be back in Cincinnati, the place they consider home."

What Education and Skills Will I Need?

High school: Preparation for junior college or four-year college.

College: Major in English, journalism, or a field that interests you and that you want to relate to public relations. Public relations people come from a wide variety of college majors, including liberal arts and the applied arts. Writing skills are mandatory.

Personal skills: Self-confidence, assertiveness, an outgoing personality, understanding of human behavior, enthusiasm, and imagination are important for success in public relations.

How Many Public Relations Workers Are There and Where Do They Work?

There are 87,000 public relations workers and half of them are working in New York, Los Angeles, Chicago, and Washington. They work for manufacturers, public utilities, transportation companies, trade and professional associations, government agencies, schools, and colleges.

$ $ $ $ $

In 1980, college graduates began in public relations from $10,000 to $13,000 a year. Within a few years with a big company, the average salary for men was $38,000 a year.

What Is the Job Future?

PR jobs are very competitive because thousands of college graduates that want to work in cities look for a job with glamour, like PR. Chances will be best for enthusiastic people with sound academic records and some media experience.

RELATED CAREERS

advertising	fundraiser
lobbyist	account executive

WHERE CAN I GET MORE INFORMATION?

Professional group
The Information Center
Public Relations Society of America, Inc.
845 Third Avenue
New York, NY 10022

Trade journals
PR Quarterly
305 East 45 Street
New York, NY 10017

Jack O'Dwyer's Newsletter
271 Madison Avenue
New York, NY 10016

BUSINESS: COMPUTER OPERATIONS

Computer Programmer
Systems Analyst

About these careers *Computer careers are expected to be the most rapidly growing occupational group in our economy through the 1980s. The world is on the verge of a computer revolution—a revolution as inevitable and sweeping in its effects as the industrial revolution. At its heart is an extraordinary development of modern technology: the microprocessor, the ultracheap, amazingly small computer that processes huge amounts of information in a fraction of a second. Christopher Evans, a renowned computer scientist, writes in his book,* The MicroMillennium, *"The computer revolution will have an overwhelming and comprehensive impact, affecting every human being on earth in every aspect of his or her life. It will run at a gallop in the next twenty-five years. Once the revolution is under way, it will be unstoppable."*

Employment in computer careers is conservatively expected to rise 85 percent in this decade. Most college graduates will be in the following jobs: systems analyst and programmer, sales, operations, and management.

Most of the growth in the computer industry will result from advances in computer capabilities. There are three major areas of new technologies: hardware—the machinery that is getting smaller, cheaper, and faster; software—the programs or instructions that tell the hardware what to do, and the language the instructions are written in; and applications—the kinds of work computers can perform.

Employment is clustered around major cities. The education and training of computer personnel will continue to be inadequate for the demand. The shortage of computer personnel is expected to continue through the 1980s, resulting in higher wages, more job mobility, increased job security, and generally greater opportunities for these workers.

On the following page is a list of professional computer job descriptions to give you an idea of what the college-level computer jobs are.

COMPUTER CAREERS

1. **Corporate Director of Data Processing:** *The top executive for all computer processing.*
2. **Technical Assistant:** *Member of corporate director's staff; usually head of advanced planning for data processing (DP) function.*
3. **Services Coordinator/User Liaison:** *Coordinates DP activities with other functions or departments.*
4. **Manager of Systems Analysis:** *Analyzes how DP can be applied to user problems; designs effective and efficient DP solutions.*
5. **Lead Systems Analyst:** *Helps plan, organize, and control the activities of the systems analysis section.*
6. **Senior Systems Analyst:** *Confers with users to define DP projects, formulates problems, and designs solutions.*
7. **Systems Analyst:** *Works with users to define DP projects or project segments, or irons out details in specifications.*
8. **Systems Analyst Trainee:** *Usually has some DP experience; expected to spend time learning rather than producing.*
9. **Manager of Applications Programming:** *Responsible for the development of effective, efficient, well-documented programs.*
10. **Lead Applications Programmer:** *Helps plan, organize, and control section activities.*
11. **Senior Applications Programmer:** *Works with program designs or specifications.*
12. **Applications Programmer:** *Works on only one or a few applications.*
13. **Applications Programmer Trainee:** *Learns to program under supervision.*
14. **Programming Team Librarian:** *Keeps track of program revisions.*
15. **Manager of System Programming:** *Plans and directs the activities of the programming section; assigns personnel to projects.*
16. **Lead Systems Programmer:** *Helps plan, organize, and control the activities of the programming section.*
17. **Senior Systems Programmer:** *Specializes in support, maintenance, and use of one or more operating systems; able to work at highest levels of programming.*
18. **Systems Programmer:** *May specialize in the support of one or a few operating system components or subsystems.*
19. **Systems Programming Trainee:** *Has a good background in DP and knows or is learning assembler language.*
20. **Program Librarian:** *Responsible for maintaining the on-line and off-line libraries of production programs in source and object form.*
21. **Manager of Data Base Administration:** *Plans, organizes, and schedules activities of the data base administration section.*
22. **Data Base Administrator:** *Analyzes company's computerized information requirements; coordinates data collection with storage needs; organizes data.*
23. **Data Communications Telecommunications Manager:** *Responsible for design of data communications networks and installation and operation of data links.*
24. **Data Communications Analyst:** *Specializes in network design, traffic analysis, and data communications software.*

COMPUTER PROGRAMMER

Writes detailed instructions called programs that list in logical order the steps the computer must follow to solve a problem.

What's It Like to Be a Computer Programmer?

There are two kinds of computer programmers: systems programmer and applications programmer. A systems programmer, sometimes called a software systems engineer, gives a particular computer the ability to perform certain tasks for a client or employer. For example, a systems programmer determines which specific computer language will be used and which functions should get priority. The applications programmer uses the language and tasks already established by the systems programmer and writes programs that tell the computers exactly what to do. An applications programmer can work quite independently and at his own pace, progressing as fast as he is capable. Most days, programmers spend an entire day writing a program for the computers, or correcting errors in one already written. In the process of designing a program system (preparing a series of programs that, for example, might keep track of production and take inventory), they may spend several hours discussing methods and details with their customers. Applications programmers often run the computers themselves, testing progress. Attending classes and lectures is important for programmers since the field is changing and growing so fast.

Earl L. King, Sr., married with a second-grade son, started as a computer programmer; he is now Manager of Data-Processing Operations for Harvard Trust Co. He is responsible for the operation of the bank's data-processing facilities. King stresses to young people that "you have to be prepared for working under close supervision at least for a year. When a programmer can handle all aspects of the job, the chances for advancement are really good. But best of all about this career is the excitement of being in on the computer revolution!"

What Education and Skills Will I Need?

High school: Preparation for college, with as much mathematics as possible.

College: Computer programmers are hired from commu-

COMPUTER PROGRAMMER

nity colleges, business colleges, two-year community colleges, and four-year colleges. Most programmers are college graduates. Major in mathematics, computer science, business, or whatever field you want to work in, such as health or engineering.

Personal skills: The work calls for patience, persistence, and the ability to be extremely accurate. Imagination and logical thinking are important for programmers who work out new solutions to problems.

How Many Computer Programmers Are There and Where Do They Work?

There are 247,000 computer programmers today and the field is expected to grow to 500,000 by 1990. Most of the jobs are clustered around major cities. Insurance companies, banks, utilities companies, and manufacturing companies hire the majority of programmers.

$ $ $ $ $

In 1980, beginning salaries for applications programmers with a college degree averaged $13,520 a year; beginning salaries for systems programmers averaged $16,380 a year. Experienced applications programmers averaged $20,800 a year, compared to about $23,920 a year for systems programmers. Lead programmers made more.

What Is the Job Future?

Opportunities are expected to increase 102 percent in the 1980s as computers are used much more in medical, educational, and data-processing services. Most of the increase will be in the high-level jobs, since the simple programming jobs are becoming automatically programmed and stored in libraries. The systems and applications programmers for complex work will be in most demand.

WHERE CAN I GET MORE INFORMATION?

Professional groups

American Federation of Information Processing Societies
210 Summit Avenue
Montvale, NJ 07645

Data Processing Management Association
505 Busse Highway
Park Ridge, IL 60068

Trade journals
Computerworld
Box 880
Framingham, MA 01701

Software News
5 Kane Industrial Drive
Hudson, MA 01749

SYSTEMS ANALYST

Decides how data is collected, prepared for the computers, processed, stored, and made available to the users.

What's It Like to Be a Systems Analyst?

Systems analysts are the problem solvers for the computer user. The systems analyst begins work by discussing with managers the jobs to be performed. He learns exactly what kind of information is needed, what has to be done with it, how quickly it has to be processed, and how it is currently being collected and recorded. In most companies, the analyst evaluates the computer equipment already owned by the company in order to determine if it can carry the additional data or if new equipment is needed. Next, the analyst develops the computer system, that is, decides how the data should be prepared for the machines, processed, stored, and made available to users. If the company decides to adopt the proposed system, the analyst prepares specifications for computer programmers to follow. Analysts usually specialize in business, scientific, or engineering applications. The problems systems analysts deal with range from monitoring nuclear fission in a power plant to forecasting sales for a publisher.

Robert D. McCaffrey, married and father of a six-year-old, is a Systems Analyst Supervisor at General Electric. His day starts with a review of the previous night's computer processing to insure that all regularly scheduled programs have run normally. Next, he reviews the progress being made on new development programs and systems to insure that schedules are being met or remedial action is being taken. Daily meetings with people who are using the data are held to discuss new development and maintenance projects. Usually, a weekly meeting is held with all programmers to review the previous week's activity and modify short-term plans if necessary. Also, meetings with management are held to review long-range plans to insure the proper resource application.

What Education and Skills Will I Need?

High school: Preparation for college, with as much mathematics as possible.

College: Systems analysts come from majors in engineering, computer science, accounting, mathematics, and economics. Regardless of the major, most must know programming language. Half of the systems analysts come from other careers and learn the necessary skills in adult and corporate education courses.

Personal skills: Ability to think logically, work with abstract ideas, and to concentrate are all needed to be a systems analyst.

How Many Systems Analysts Are There and Where Do They Work?

There are 205,000 systems analysts and that number is expected to grow to 400,000 by 1990. Most of them started as computer programmers and advanced to systems analysts. They work for manufacturing firms, banks, and insurance companies in urban areas clustered around major cities.

$ $ $ $ $

In 1980, beginning systems analysts started at $17,000 a year; experienced analysts earned $24,000 a year; lead analysts made from $24,500 to $25,750 a year.

What Is the Job Future?

Sophisticated accounting systems, telecommunications networks, and scientific research have resulted in new approaches to problem solving. Jobs will increase 120 percent through the 1980s. Opportunities will be especially good in medical, educational and data-processing services.

WHERE CAN I GET MORE INFORMATION?

Professional group
American Federation of Information Processing Societies
1815 North Lynn Street
Arlington, VA 22209

Trade journals
Computerworld
Box 880
Framingham, MA 01701

Software News
5 Kane Industrial Drive
Hudson, MA 01749

BUSINESS: MONEY MANAGEMENT

Accountant
Actuary
Bank Officer
Credit Manager

About these careers *There are over one and a half million jobs in these four money-management careers, most of them held by men.*

Money management requires a college education, and for banking, a well-organized officer-training program ranging from six months to one year is the best preparation. Bank trainees may start as credit or investment analysts, or may rotate among bank departments to get the "feel" of banking.

Advancement in money management depends largely on job performance and the qualifying examinations in accounting and actuary work, which require specialized study. Courses in every phase of banking are offered by the American Institute of Banking, an industry-sponsored school.

Money managers work in well-lighted, attractive, comfortable offices. Since a great deal of bank business and credit business depends on customers' impressions, money managers are encouraged to wear conservative, somewhat formal, business clothes. Most jobs require no travel, although accountants employed by national accounting firms may travel extensively to conduct audits and perform other services for their clients. Most money managers work overtime at home, and some are constantly studying at home for the qualifying examinations necessary for advancement. The first ten years in a money-management career limits the time for social and family life outside of work.

ACCOUNTANT

Designs and controls financial records and analyzes financial data.

What's It Like to Be an Accountant?

Marcel Renaud, Certified Public Accountant (CPA), says it takes a special person to be an accountant. "Figures are three meals a day for an accountant and study never stops. It's a science and you must keep up-to-date, reading three to five hours a week." Accountants prepare financial reports, profit and loss studies, cost studies, and tax reports. The three major fields are public, management, and government accounting. Public accountants are independent and work for themselves on a fee basis for businesses or individuals, or for an accounting firm. Management accountants, also called industrial or private accountants, handle the financial records of a company and work on a salary basis. Government accountants examine financial records of government agencies and audit private businesses for government regulations. Any of these accountants may specialize in auditing, taxes, cost accounting, investing, budgeting and control, information processing, or systems and procedures.

What Education and Skills Will I Need?

High school: A college preparatory program with strong interest and ability in mathematics is necessary for a Certified Public Accountant program. Alternatives include a commercial course leading to a business college program or community college program in accounting, correspondence study in accounting, or a college course leading to a business administration major.

College: Accounting is offered in a one-year business college program, two-year community college program, and four-year college program. Nine out of ten CPAs are college graduates, have passed the CPA examination in the state in which they work, and have had two years of accounting experience before taking the exam. In the near future, some states may require CPA candidates to have a graduate degree, and computer programming skills are increasingly required.

Personal skills: Aptitude for mathematics, ability to work independently; good at working with systems and computers; accuracy; and a high standard of integrity are necessary in an accounting career.

How Many Accountants Are There and Where Do They Work?

Twenty percent of the 900,000 accountants are Certified Public Accountants. About 75 percent of all accountants are men. Sixty percent are in management accounting, while others work in their own firms or for the government. Most accountants work in urban centers where there are large accounting firms and central offices of big businesses.

$ $ $ $ $

In 1980, starting salaries for accountants averaged $16,800 a year. Beginners with a master's degree started at $19,200 a year. Accountants with experience made from $18,400 to $31,900 a year, and chief accountants made from $28,300 to $50,000 a year.

What Is the Job Future?

The 1980s are the decade of the accountant. New tax laws and increased pressure on businesses to improve budgeting and accounting procedures will provide all kinds of jobs. Employment for both college graduates and noncollege graduates will be excellent through the 1980s. Big businesses prefer college graduates who have worked part-time while in school. Those who specialize in a specific phase of accounting will find the best career opportunities.

RELATED CAREERS

appraiser	loan officer
budget officer	financial analyst

WHERE CAN I GET MORE INFORMATION?

Professional groups

National Association of Accountants
919 Third Avenue
New York, NY 10022

National Society of Public Accountants
1717 Pennsylvania Avenue, NW
Washington, D.C. 20006

Trade journal
Journal of Accountancy
American Institute of CPA
666 Fifth Avenue
New York, NY 10019

ACTUARY

Assembles and analyzes statistics in order to design insurance and pension plans on a profit-making basis.

What's It Like to Be an Actuary?

Why do teenage boys pay more for car insurance? How much is a life insurance policy for a 21-year-old male? Answers to these and similar questions are provided by actuaries. Actuaries calculate probabilities of death, sickness, injury, disability, unemployment, retirement, and property loss from accident, theft, and fire. They use statistics to construct probability tables in order to develop insurance rates. They usually work for a life insurance or liability insurance company. Mark Magnus, a young, single actuary in a Boston insurance company, reviews actuarial information for pension plans. This involves making sure that employers invest enough money wisely for retired workers to get a monthly pension for life. Magnus warns young men that the home study for the required actuarial examination takes 15 to 25 hours a week and really cuts down on social and family life.

What Education and Skills Will I Need?

High school: College preparatory course, with as much mathematics as possible.

College: A degree is required, with a good background in calculus, probability and statistics, and computer science. Major in mathematics, statistics, economics, or business administration. While still in college, you should begin to take the examinations required to become a professional actuary; it takes from 5 to 10 years to complete the exams after college while on the job. There are 17 colleges and universities who offer special training for actuarial careers.

Personal skills: Mathematical skills, interest in study and working independently to pass examinations on your own, and ability to do routine detailed work are needed.

How Many Actuaries Are There and Where Do They Work?

There are 10,700 professional actuaries in the U.S. and most of them are men. Almost half are employed in the five cities with major insurance industries, which include New York, Hartford, Chicago, Philadelphia, and Boston. Private insurance companies employ 90 percent of all actuaries.

$ $ $ $ $

In 1980, starting salaries for college graduates without passing any actuarial exams averaged $13,000 a year. The pay increases rapidly as the actuarial exams are passed. Beginners who have passed one exam started at $17,000 a year; those who passed two exams started at $18,000.

What Is the Job Future?

Opportunities are expected to be very good through the 1980s. Because of the rising numbers of insurance policies of all kinds, and the expanding group health and life plans, employment in the actuarial field will increase as the health occupations increase. "The best jobs and most money go to the graduates who have passed two or more actuary examinations while they are still in college," writes Mark Magnus.

RELATED CAREERS

mathematician
statistician
economist
financial analyst
engineering analyst

WHERE CAN I GET MORE INFORMATION?

Professional groups
Society of Actuaries
208 South La Salle Street
Chicago, IL 60604

Casualty Actuarial Society
One Penn Plaza
250 West 34 Street
New York, NY 10019

Trade journal
Risk Management
205 East 42 Street
New York, NY 10017

BANK OFFICER

Banks are in the "money" business and bank officers are responsible for the management of the bank's business.

What's It Like to Be a Bank Officer?

Officers in a bank include the loan officer, who makes decisions on loan applications within the policy of the bank; trust officer, who manages property, funds, or real estate for clients, including financial planning, investment, and taxes; operations officer, who manages efficient procedures of the bank; customer manager, who is responsible for relations with customers and other banks; branch bank manager, who has full responsibility for a branch office; personnel administrator; and public relations and operational research officers. Ian Burnham, a management trainee in a major California bank, began his career with a six-month course at the American Institute of Banking after graduating in economics from a liberal arts college. He is single and lives with a woman who is also in the training program. The only investment they have made in furniture is a basic home computer, which sits right in the middle of their living room. Burnham likes the conservative style of banking, business clothes, and formal offices. He is especially interested in new tax structures and pension plans, with their investment implications for a large number of bank customers. "If you're interested in money management," says Burnham, "a bank-training program is a good place to learn."

What Education and Skills Will I Need?

High school: Preparation for college, with emphasis on mathematics and economics.

College: Many bank officers major in business administration, accounting, or economics; some major in finance and banking. The large city banks have training programs especially for liberal arts graduates who are interested in finance, regardless of their college major. A Master of Business Administration (MBA) with computer skills is an "ideal education" for future bank managers.

Personal skills: Ability to analyze detailed information, good judgment for advising others, and tact are needed in banking.

How Many Bankers Are There and Where Do They Work?

Of the 400,000 bank officers, 320,000 are men and most are Caucasian. They work in every bank in the country—from rural banking to big city banking with well-developed training programs for executives.

$ $ $ $ $

In 1980, beginning college graduates in officer training programs of large banks started from $1,100 to $1,300 a month. Those with a master's degree started from $1,300 to $1,900 a month; and those with an MBA started from $1,400 to $2,400 a month. The officers of small town banks work up from tellers and are paid much less than city bankers.

What Is the Job Future?

Chances for work as a bank officer will be competitive through the 1980s. More services and a greater use of computers will require sound management and more jobs, but the number of applicants has increased. Promotions from junior to senior officers will be as competitive as they have always been.

RELATED CAREERS

industrial relations director
city manager
any business management career

WHERE CAN I GET MORE INFORMATION?

Professional group
American Bankers Association
1120 Connecticut Avenue, NW
Washington, D.C. 20036

Trade journal
American Banker
525 West 42 Street
New York, NY 10036

CREDIT MANAGER

Decides which individuals or businesses are eligible for credit, according to a credit policy.

What's It Like to Be a Credit Manager?

Coins and paper money are on the way out. Computerized credit is on its way in. Soon, credit managers will be dealing with how to identify the owners of credit through a special watch worn to monitor their blood pressure, pulse, or electric skin resistance. In the meantime, credit managers decide who can receive credit by analyzing detailed financial reports of businesses (commercial credit) or bank records, credit bureau recommendations, and applications of individuals (consumer credit). They are also responsible for establishing the company's credit policy and setting financial standards on the basis of the amount of risk the company can take. They often work with salespeople in developing the company's credit policy.

What Education and Skills Will I Need?

High school: Preparation for a two-year or a four-year college.

College: Most credit managers have a college degree in business administration, accounting, or economics in order to get into the good training programs. Others have finished a two-year accounting or business administration program. Understanding computer systems is crucial for all career levels in credit.

Personal skills: Ability to analyze details and draw logical conclusions, a pleasant personality, and speaking skills are necessary for success as a credit manager.

How Many Credit Managers Are There and Where Do They Work?

Of the 55,000 credit managers, 60 percent are men. Most work in urban areas in the U.S. About half work for wholesale and retail trade, and one-third work for manufacturers and banks.

$ $ $ $ $

In 1980, trainees with a college degree started at $12,000 to $14,000 a year. Experienced credit managers averaged from $22,000 to $25,000 a year. The top-level jobs paid over $40,000 a year.

What Is the Job Future?

Jobs are competitive in credit management through the 1980s. Credit has increased very rapidly and is here to stay. As firms strive to get the biggest sales of their products and services, there will be a greater demand for skilled credit managers who can establish credit policies strict enough to minimize bad debt losses. Use of computers, telecommunications networks, and centralized credit will limit the growth of jobs.

RELATED CAREERS

loan officer
credit union manager
controller
financial institution manager

CREDIT MANAGER

WHERE CAN I GET MORE INFORMATION?

Professional group
National Association of Credit Management
475 Park Avenue South
New York, NY 10016

Trade journal
Credit and Finance Management
475 Park Avenue South
New York, NY 10016

BUSINESS: SALES

Automobile Salesperson
Insurance Salesperson
Manufacturer's Salesperson
Real Estate Salesperson
Stockbroker
Travel Agent

About these careers *In sales jobs, you can make the most amount of money for the least amount of education. However, high unemployment rates and tough competition for jobs have increased the need for a college degree to get into some sales training programs. There are 6.8 million salespeople and .9 million, or 16 percent, of them have a college degree. Most salespeople come from a great variety of college backgrounds, although manufacturers' salespeople often come from technical or scientific backgrounds.*

Beginning salespeople work evenings, weekends, and holidays — whenever the customers and clients are free to buy. Some manufacturers' salespeople have large territories and travel a lot. Others usually work in the neighborhood of their "home base." The amount of time a beginning salesperson puts into building up his accounts is inconvenient for his family and friends. But, once these accounts are established, which takes about ten years or so, he can meet his clients at their mutual convenience — on the golf course, on the racquetball court, or at lunch.

If you are interested in sales and have decided not to go for the big money, then you can put in fewer hours because salespeople are free to set up their own time schedule. More than 25 percent of the 6.8 million people in sales work part-time. Sales work provides many opportunities for coordinating a career with parenting, which many parents need until their children are older.

Salespeople who have managerial ability may advance to assistant sales manager, sales manager, or general manager. Some managers open their own businesses or become partners in dealerships or agencies and firms. Most sales advancement is in terms of making more money and having more free time as customer accounts become well-established.

AUTOMOBILE SALESPERSON

Sells new and used cars for car dealers.

What's It Like to Be an Automobile Salesperson?

An automobile salesperson must know about *selling,* not about the complicated details of the product. The main thing is to know how to close a deal, that is, overcome the customer's hesitancy to buy. Often, a new salesperson begins a sale and an experienced one helps close the sale. A new salesperson may quote prices and then must learn how to give a trade-in allowance for the customer's present car. The salesperson often arranges financing and insurance for the cars he sells. Good salespeople develop and follow leads of prospective customers. Car selling is an exciting job because you deal with $300 to $500 profit on each car you sell.

Jim Donovan, a young married man with three children, sells strictly on commission. He says what he likes best about the job is that he is his own boss, the job pays well if you put the time into it, and it is rewarding to see a satisfied customer on the day of delivery. "The fact that someone has had enough confidence in you for a seven- or eight-thousand dollar purchase makes you feel good."

What Education and Skills Will I Need?

High school: Most salespeople have a high school diploma. They are usually trained on the job by sales managers and experienced salespeople.

College: Many new car dealers have some college, but business and selling experience counts more than a degree.

Personal skills: Sales skills, initiative, assertiveness, enthusiasm for the product, and ambition make a successful salesworker.

How Many Automobile Salespeople Are There and Where Do They Work?

There are an estimated 157,000 automobile salespeople and 114,000 work for new car dealers. They work in every city, town, and village in the country. New car dealers employ from one to 50 salespeople.

$ $ $ $ $

In 1980, salespeople in the automobile business averaged $18,000 a year. Earnings vary widely depending on geography, experience, and type and size of dealership.

What Is the Job Future?

With the energy crisis upon us, unemployment in Detroit, and a recession, all related car jobs are going to be hard to predict. Anyone who can prove himself a seller can convince a dealer to hire him for a commission job that doesn't involve a financial risk to the dealer. If selling cars is what you want to do, you can suggest a plan to a dealer (after hours on another job, or after school, or week-ends). Ask for a few months' trial, and if the dealer makes money, you will have a job.

RELATED CAREERS

insurance agent
manufacturer's salesperson
real estate agent
stockbroker

WHERE CAN I GET MORE INFORMATION?

Professional group
National Automobile Dealers Association
8400 Westpark Drive
McLean, VA 22102

Trade journal
Automobile News
965 East Jefferson
Detroit, MI 48207

INSURANCE SALESPERSON

Sells policies that protect individuals and businesses against future losses and financial pressures.

What's It Like to Be an Insurance Salesperson?

There are 1.6 million people in the insurance field and one-third of them are in sales. Other insurance jobs for college graduates include managers, underwriters, and actuaries. An insurance agent sells for one company, usually on a commission basis; a broker sells insurance for several companies. Managers are responsible for the administration of policy accounting, investments, and loans. Underwriters review insurance applications to evaluate the risk involved in order to determine profit for the company. Accountants, bookkeepers, and lawyers are also employed by insurance companies.

John E. Wilson, Jr., business executive for the John Hancock Mutual Life Insurance Company, likes the interaction with people best about his work. He likes motivating, guiding, and producing an end result. Wilson thinks it is important for students to realize that many interests or circumstances develop during a career that bring changes they might not plan or intend. He would like to see young people plan their education with more flexibility than most think is needed. "Our top insurance sales and management people, for example, come from a great variety of college majors and work experiences. Their skills would lead them to excel in sales and management in any number of other fields, as well."

What Education and Skills Will I Need?

High school: Preparation for business, junior, or four-year college.

College: Major in business administration, personnel, insurance, or liberal arts. Insurance salespeople come from all kinds of educational backgrounds, and a degree is not a necessity for sales jobs. All agents and most brokers must be licensed in the state where they plan to sell insurance. You can qualify for many good insurance jobs through correspondence courses in insurance.

Personal skills: Depending on the job, the sales skills or management or business skills needed for any big business are needed in insurance.

How Many Insurance Salespeople Are There and Where Do They Work?

There are 325,000 full time insurance agents and brokers. One-ninth of the insurance jobs are managerial and one-fifteenth are professional. Every town has agents and brokers, and the "home office" people are in the insurance centers of the country: California, Connecticut, Illinois, Massachusetts, New Jersey, New York, and Texas.

$ $ $ $ $

Beginners start at a salary of about $1,000 a month for six months before they go on commission. Brokers work on commission. After five years of building a clientele, salespeople had a median income of $22,000 a year in 1981. Top agents made $40,000 a year and many earned over $100,000 a year.

What Is the Job Future?

The selling business is a competitive field, with many turnovers for beginning salespeople. Selling is a good opportunity for people who are ambitious and who enjoy saleswork. Opportunities in middle management will continue to be good, as the insurance industry is expected to rise moderately.

RELATED CAREERS

real estate agent
car sales
manufacturer's company representative
stockbroker

WHERE CAN I GET MORE INFORMATION?

Professional group
Insurance Information Institute
110 William Street
New York, NY 10038

Trade journals
The Insurance Salesman
1200 North Meridan Street
Indianapolis, IN 46206

Insurance Week
2322 Seattle First National Bank Building
Seattle, WA 98154

MANUFACTURER'S SALESPERSON

Sells all manufactured products, mainly to businesses and institutions.

What's It Like to Be a Manufacturer's Salesperson?

A manufacturer's salesperson, sometimes called a sales engineer or industrial salesperson, spends most of his time visiting prospective customers. He also reports on sales and customers' credit rating, plans sales schedules, makes up lists of new customers, handles correspondence, and studies the company's product. Some salespersons promote their product by displays at conferences or by giving demonstrations to companies on how to use their products.

What Education and Skills Will I Need?

High school: Preparation for college. College graduates are preferred.

College: Many technical or specialized salespersons are engineers, pharmacists, or chemists. Others come from business or liberal arts majors. Computer skills are necessary for all salespersons.

Personal skills: Selling skills, assertiveness, a pleasant appearance, interest in the product, and the ability to get along well with people are needed to be a salesperson.

MANUFACTURER'S SALESPERSON

How Many Manufacturers' Salespeople Are There and Where Do They Work?

There are 440,000 salespeople, mostly men. More work for food companies than any other industry. Large numbers also work for printing and publishing, chemicals, drugs, metal products, and electrical and machinery industries.

$ $ $ $ $

In 1980, beginners averaged from $13,900 to $15,400 a year. The highest salaries were in electrical and electronics equipment, construction materials, hardware and tools, and scientific and precision instruments. The majority of salesworkers get paid on a combination of salary, commission, and bonus, earning between $21,000 and $24,000 a year with experience.

What Is the Job Future?

Jobs will be good for well-trained and ambitious people through the 1980s.

RELATED CAREERS

real estate agent	retail buyer
car salesperson	stockbroker

WHERE CAN I GET MORE INFORMATION?

Professional group
Manufacturers' Agents National Association
P.O. Box 16878
Irvine, CA 92713

Trade journal
The American Salesman
424 North 3 Street
Burlington, IA 52601

REAL ESTATE SALESPERSON

Represents property owners who want to sell or rent residential and commercial properties.

What's It Like to Be in Real Estate?

Real estate salespeople show and sell real estate; most handle rental properties as well. Bill Rosen, a Boston Beacon-Hill agent, works from 9 a.m. to 7 p.m. analyzing mail and "listing books" for new properties, showing clients apartments for sale or rent, and making calls for new listings. "Real estate is a constantly changing business—no two days are the same," says Rosen, "but you have to accept the frustration of working hard on a sale and having it fall through at the last minute. Matching property to people can be very rewarding," continues Rosen, "and each year of experience sharpens your skill in learning exactly what people want." Rosen is single and finds that the excitement and complexities in his work are enough for him.

Commercial real estate is where the big money and risks are. At 35 years of age, Donald Trump is New York City's real estate "genius." He is a promoter who matches would-be buyers with sellers, arranges financing, and paves the administrative way for big projects—and in the process gains an ownership stake for himself. Trump graduated from military school and the Wharton School of Finance before he started working for his father, refinancing 5,000 apartment units in New York's Brooklyn and Queens. He is married to a woman who skied on the 1972 Austrian Olympic Team. According to the *Wall Street Journal,* Trump is known to have made the "tax deal of the century" with New York City for his client. He is currently working on a $1.5 billion real estate deal, the World Trade Center, which would make the biggest real estate transaction ever.

What Education and Skills Will I Need?

A college degree is not required in order to be a real estate salesperson or broker, although a state real estate license is required. More than 200 colleges and many correspondence schools offer one or more courses in real estate to qualify for the real estate examination. Ability to sell is the key to success in real estate careers.

Personal skills: Pleasant personality, assertiveness, enthusiasm, tact, a good memory for faces and names, and a neat appearance are necessary for successful saleswork.

How Many Real Estate Salespeople Are There and Where Do They Work?

There are 520,000 full-time real estate salespeople. Part-time people in real estate outnumber full-time, and in 1980 there were 4 million licensed realtors. Most real estate salespeople are in small businesses and are self-employed.

$ $ $ $ $

Commissions on sales are the means of income in the real estate business. Commissions vary from 5 to 10 percent, depending on the type of property and the part of the country. In 1980, full-time real estate agents earned an average of $14,700 a year. Experienced salespeople make much more than that.

What Is the Job Future?

Jobs in real estate are very competitive and will continue to be so. Shifts in the population ages that need housing will create more jobs. The best chances for work will go to the well-trained, ambitious people who enjoy selling. The high cost of mortgages has resulted in a tough real estate situation so far during the economic recession of the early 1980s.

RELATED CAREERS

car salesperson
insurance salesperson
securities salesperson
manufacturer's representative

WHERE CAN I GET MORE INFORMATION?

Professional group
National Association of Realtors
430 North Michigan Avenue
Chicago, IL 60611

Trade journals
The Appraisal Journal
NAREB
155 East Superior Street
Chicago, IL 60611

The Wall Street Journal
Dow Jones
30 Broad Street
New York, NY 10004

STOCKBROKER

Sells stocks, bonds, or mutual funds to individuals and institutions.

What's It Like to Be a Stockbroker?

A stockbroker, sometimes called a securities salesperson, gets an order for stock and relays the order through the firm's order room to the floor of a securities exchange or his firm's trading department. After this transaction is completed, the stockbroker notifies the customer of the sale. Other duties of the broker include explaining the stock market and trading practices to customers, suggesting when to buy and when to sell, and often managing the money of institutions with millions of dollars to invest.

West Point graduate Michael Johnson is a stockbroker with Merrill Lynch, Pierce, Fenner & Smith. He is in his twenties, with a wife, child, and new baby due. Johnson says that the hours are long when you get started because you have to build up your own accounts; but he loves the money and the freedom to organize his day in any way that he wants. "I look forward to my future, when my clients are well-established and I can meet them on the golf course like the brokers who have 'made it,'" says Johnson.

Argie Economou, Associate Vice-president with Dean Witter Reynolds, didn't even know what a stockbroker was after three years in premedicine, one year in economics, and one year in the corporate world before he served in the Vietnam War. He watched a young stockbroker who was an Army Second Lieutenant persuade the men to invest their money rather than throw it away. When he returned to the corporate world, he found he had been bitten by the bug of finance and investments. In 1970, he was offered a job in New York. His training included 6 months at the New York Institute of Finance and a lot of backroom paper work and study at E. F. Hutton, his first job. After ten years in the business, despite the valleys and peaks, he wouldn't be anywhere else. "I'm my own boss," explains Economou. "I can come and go as I please. I can make 126 phone calls in one day as I did in November 1973, the all-time low since I've been here, or I can take off and make none. It's a moving business of endless variety. Everything you see in this world – everything you see or smell or touch relates to business. It's all consuming and I love it."

Marcus Freidlander, 77, former Trading Specialist on the New York Stock Exchange and currently Money Management Consultant on Madison Avenue, says the business is changing. "People need more and more general money management from their broker, but as long as the broker makes money only on commission from the sale of stocks and bonds, there is going to be a frustrating situation for everybody. The demand for broader advice from a broker won't change, so the job and the way the service is paid has to be different."

What Education and Skills Will I Need?

High school: Preparation for college. You should read the financial pages of newspapers in order to learn about daily financial situations, especially the Sunday business sections of *The New York Times* and *The Wall Street Journal.*

College: Almost all trainees for stockbrokerage firms are college graduates. They come from many liberal arts majors, although economics and prelaw are the predominant college majors.

Personal skills: Selling skills, interest in making money and in the financial world, and ambition are needed for success in stocks.

How Many Stockbrokers Are There and Where Do They Work?

There are 63,000 full-time stockbrokers and another 63,000 who work part-time. They are employed by brokerage firms, investment bankers, and mutual funds firms. Most brokers work for a few large firms who have offices in large and small cities all over the country.

$ $ $ $ $

Trainees start at $900 to $1,200 a month, depending on the size of the firm, until they are licensed and working on commission. In 1980, full-time stockbrokers who sell to individuals averaged $40,000 a year, while brokers selling to institutions averaged over $88,000 a year.

What Is the Job Future?

Jobs will be competitive, but there will be jobs for well-trained successful salespeople. During a recession, jobs are few and commissions low, but in the future the opportunities will be good. Johnson of Merrill Lynch advises young men to get 2 to 3 years of successful business experience before they apply for a training program with a major investment firm.

RELATED CAREERS

insurance agent
real estate agent
commodities broker
securities trader

WHERE CAN I GET MORE INFORMATION?

Professional groups

New York Stock Exchange
11 Wall Street
New York, NY 10005

Securities Industry Association
20 Broad Street
New York, NY 10005

Trade journal

Wall Street Journal
Dow Jones
30 Broad Street
New York, NY 10004

TRAVEL AGENT

Organizes, schedules, and sells travel services to the public.

What's It Like to Be a Travel Agent?

The travel agent is a dealer in dreams, other people's dreams, and in the course of a day he plans many round-the-world trips, vacations, special event trips, as well as the routine business trips for regular customers. An agent must possess a great deal of specialized knowledge about the climate, accommodations, fares, places of interest, tariffs and customs laws, currency exchange, and sources of references for new information. When an anthropologist schedules a trip to Taute, New Guinea, the agent must supply exact information about connections and time changes from airline to airline and time zone to time zone. The agent must know that when the anthropologist ends up in a mission plane in Lumi, walking through the bush is the only means of transportation left to get to his or her destination! Travel agencies are service agencies. Good will and good client relations are vitally important to making a profit in these services. Knowing details, excursion rates, and suggestions for making trips convenient and comfortable are imperative for a successful agent.

What Education and Skills Will I Need?

Most travel agents have some college background, although it is not a requirement. Courses in geography, history, and a foreign language are helpful. Some travel agents take travel agency courses that are offered in special schools and correspondence schools; other travel agents learn while on the job.

Personal skills: Sales skills, business ability, interest in details and accuracy, and a pleasant personality that can accept people changing their plans are necessary to be successful as a travel agent.

How Many Travel Agents Are There and Where Do They Work?

There are 52,000 travel agents in the U.S. and Canada. About one-fourth of the agents are self-employed. Most agencies hire from one to 40 agents, with about half men. The urban and resort areas employ the most number of agents.

$ $ $ $ $

Beginners start low, as the jobs are competitive and so many young people want to work in the travel industry. In 1980, agents averaged from $9,500 to $18,000 a year. Owners of their own business make 5 percent on domestic travel, 10 percent on international travel, and 10 percent on cruises and hotels. Young people often go into this career for the fringe benefits, which include vacations at reduced rates, and transportation and hotels at a discount when they travel. Often, agents are invited for free holidays to see and recommend the facilities of an airline or resort hotel.

What Is the Job Future?

The travel industry is a very competitive field, since it is one of the glamour careers that many qualified people apply to each year. The surest way to get a start in the travel industry is to take any job any small agency offers you and work toward a promotion after learning the job.

RELATED CAREERS

airline reservations agent
rental car agent
town guide
salesperson

WHERE CAN I GET MORE INFORMATION?

Professional group
American Society of Travel Agents
711 Fifth Avenue
New York, NY 10022

Trade journal
Travel Trade
605 Fifth Avenue
New York, NY 10017

COMMUNICATIONS

Cable TV
Radio Broadcasting
Television Broadcasting
Writer

About these careers *Responses such as, "I'm a writer," or "I'm in TV," to the question, "What do you do for work?" almost always evoke envy. Communications careers are glamorous, and because they are, competition for most jobs is tough, with many more jobseekers than there are job openings. Some people are attracted by the image of media jobs — the opportunities to meet public figures, to appear before nationwide audiences, to attend special events. It is often difficult to see the hard work required when looking at the glamorous aspects of communications careers.*

Communications is a process that begins with observing what is happening, analyzing and interpreting that information, and transmitting it to an audience through a variety of media. The field includes a broad range of careers that have to do with research, writing, editing, and production; it encompasses educational, medical, business, speech, joke, screen, and fiction writing; and interpreting, translating, public relations, advertising, and many other specialties.

Specialties that take the place of mass media are becoming the new media. The three major television networks have lost viewers to cable television with its 30 choices in all kinds of specialties that a viewer can watch with just the flip of a switch at any time of day or night. Big newspapers are closing while small specialized local newspapers and magazines are thriving. Specialization means more jobs that require more depth of knowledge in particular areas.

The intellectual skills acquired during college are important for a communications career. Acute powers of observation and the ability to think clearly and logically are necessary traits, because people in communications need to understand the significance of the events they observe. A feeling for language enables newspaper reporters and broadcast journalists to breathe life and meaning into the overwhelming number of events that occur every day. A knack for drama through the spoken word makes radio and television announcers attractive to audiences of all kinds. Even though the competition is tough, there will be jobs through the 1980s for talented people who have acquired appropriate education and experience. The willingness to "start at the bottom" will help get the job. A combination of talent, education, motivation, imagination, and "luck" helps too.

CABLE TV

Plans, prepares, produces, and sells cable television programs.

What's It Like to Be in Cable TV?

"You have to be hungry, ambitious, and energetic to compete in this industry," says Vivian Horner, Vice-president of program development for Warner Amex Cable in New York. Cable television is the fastest growing communications career in the country. It reaches into 14.5 million American homes, according to Toffler's *The Third Wave,* and "is likely to spread with hurricane force in the early 1980s." Industry experts expect 20 to 26 million cable TV subscribers by the mid-1980s. As in most new and expanding industries, many jobs are being created where none existed before. The fierce competition in cable TV today is in winning the franchise (exclusive right) to deliver cable in cities, towns, and boroughs. When a cable company is competing for franchise rights, from 10 to 50 people may be working to study the locality and prepare a bid. The franchise team must determine the needs of a community and develop a responsive programming package. "Working on a franchise team is a good way to enter and learn the industry," says J. Carroll, Director of Franchise Proposals at Warner Amex Cable. However, in a few years when most cities become franchised, there will no longer be a need for the team. Other major jobs in cable TV are the same as those in broadcasting: marketing, sales, and operations.

After graduation from Oberlin, Mark Irish headed for New York City and cable TV and landed a job at Showtime. His whole life is wrapped up in his work, which often lasts until 7 or 8 P.M. in the office, followed by a viewing of a film later in the evening, where "everyone" in the industry has to be seen. "A social life is almost impossible unless you take your date to work to the viewings," says Irish. "This life is just as crazy and glamorous and tough as they say it is. I love it. I wouldn't be anywhere else —except Los Angeles—doing the same thing."

What Education and Skills Will I Need?

High school: Preparation for college and a communications major, with as much writing, speaking, and reading as you can get in high school.

College: Major in communications, radio and television, journalism, theater arts, business, or a related area.

Personal skills: A well-modulated speaking voice, a reasonable command of the English language, plus knowledge of dramatics, sports, music, and current events are important for the entertainment side of cable TV. Programming careers require an interest in business and detail, as well.

How Many Cable TV Workers Are There and Where Do They Work?

There are 34,000 jobs in the cable TV industry and the jobs are clustered around major cities. Cable employment projections are that the current number will more than double in the 1980s to over 65,000 jobs.

$ $ $ $ $

Members of a franchise team for a major cable TV company make from $25,000 to $40,000 a year. Selling is an important job in cable, as subscriber fees are the major source of income. Entry-level salaries range from $12,000 to $20,000 in sales, depending on geographic location. Experienced account executives can earn over $30,000. Operations is the business-management side of the cable TV industry. An operations manager oversees capital expenditures, customer service, accounts payable and receivable, installation and maintenance, and other administrative functions. Salaries for entry-level operations range from $12,000 to $15,000 in small systems and go over $60,000 in major cities.

What Is the Job Future?

Along with computers, cable television is the fastest growing industry of the 1980s. As in other communications fields, it is a glamorous career with many talented and ambitious young people applying for jobs. Working in a ground-level industry is a wonderful opportunity to learn with the growth of the industry.

RELATED CAREERS

commercial and public radio
commercial and public television
business management
sales

WHERE CAN I GET MORE INFORMATION?

Professional group
The National Cable Television Association
918 16th Street, NW
Washington, D.C. 20006

Trade journals
CableVision
Titsch Publishing, Inc.
1130 Delaware Plaza, P.O. Box 4305
Denver, CO 80204

Multi-Channel News
Fairchild Publications, Inc.
P.O. Box 18248
Denver, CO 80218

THE TOP TEN CABLE COMPANIES

Teleprompter Cable TV
888 Seventh Avenue
New York, NY 10019

American Television and Communications Corp.
160 Inverness Drive, W
Englewood, CO 80150

Tele-Communications, Inc.
5455 S. Valencia Way
Denver, CO 80222

Cox Cable Communications
219 Perimeter Center Parkway
Atlanta, GA 30346

Warner Amex Cable Communications, Inc.
75 Rockefeller Plaza
New York, NY 10019

The Times Mirror Co.
Times Mirror Square
Los Angeles, CA 90053

Storer Broadcasting Co.
1177 Kane Concourse
Miami Beach, FL 33154

Viacom International
1211 Ave. of Americas
New York, NY 10036

Sammons Communications
Box 225728
Dallas, TX 75265

UA-Columbia Cablevision
315 Post Road, W
Westport, CT 06880

RADIO AND TELEVISION BROADCASTING

Plans, prepares, produces, and presents radio and television programs.

What's It Like to Be in Radio and Television Broadcasting?

The glamor and excitement of radio and television make broadcasting careers attractive to about 200,000 people who are employed in this career. Whether in commercial or public broadcasting, *radio and television directors* plan and supervise individual programs or series of programs. They coordinate the shows, select artists and studio personnel, schedule and conduct rehearsals, and direct on-the-air shows. They are often assisted by entry-level associates who arrange details, distribute scripts and changes in scripts to the cast, and help direct shows. They also may arrange for props, makeup service, artwork, and film slides, and help with timing. *Announcers* probably are the best known workers in the industry. They introduce programs, guests, and musical selections and deliver most of the live commercials. In small stations, they also may operate the control board, sell time, and write commercial and news copy. *Musical directors* select, arrange, and direct music for programs following general instructions from program directors. News gathering and reporting are another key aspect of radio and television programming. *News directors* plan and supervise all news and special events coverage. *News reporters* gather and analyze information about newsworthy events for broadcast on radio or TV programs. They may specialize in a particular field, such as economics, health, or foreign affairs, and often report special news events from the scene. *News writers* select and write copy for newscasters to read on the air. In many stations, the jobs of newswriter and newscaster are combined. In addition, broadcasting stations have video and film editors, engineering technicians, a sales department who sells time to advertisers that sponsor the programs, and a general administration department.

A radio and TV announcer who came to the media from public relations work with U.S. Senator Patrick Leahy (D–Vt.), Jack Berry hosts his own radio show every morning and an educational TV talk show about public affairs every weeknight.

Divorced and father of three children, Berry urges young men to start as early as possible to get experience, even if it's for no pay. In such a competitive field, any experience counts in getting the few jobs available. Berry spends a lot of time preparing for his shows and keeping up with current events to get new ideas about people and issues to feature on his programs. He recruits people to interview and reads their books or other material about their work so that his interviews on radio or TV are as perceptive as they can be.

Frank Mankiewicz, President of National Public Radio, has put NPR on the map in his short four years with them. He has expanded the network budget from $8 million to $14 million, with an additional $17 million going directly to the stations. Mankiewicz's first goal was to strengthen the network's news coverage. He increased the news to three and a half hours a day, which is more than any other broadcast medium except the all-news stations. Ideally, he says, the future will bring more new stations with greater diversity.

What Education and Skills Will I Need?

High school: Preparation for liberal arts college or a communications major, with as much writing, speaking, and reading as you can get in high school.

College: Major in liberal arts, communications, radio and television, journalism, theater arts, or a related area.

Personal skills. A well-modulated speaking voice, a reasonable command of the English language, plus knowledge of dramatics, sports, music, and current events are important. Careers in announcing require a dramatic personality with special style. Programming careers require an interest in business and detail as well.

How Many Radio and Television Workers Are There and Where Do They Work?

There are 19,000 full-time announcers in radio and television, and 120,000 full-time and 30,000 part-time staff employed in commercial broadcasting; half are in radio. They work in 7,000 commercial radio stations and 700 commercial television stations in the U.S. In addition, there are 700 educational radio stations and 220 educational television stations. There are also 3,150 cable TV systems who hire about 9,500 workers.

$ $ $ $ $

In 1980, beginning announcers made from $150 to $160 a week in small stations. With experience, they made from $225 to $350 a week. Salaries in public broadcasting still are not competitive with commercial broadcasting.

What Is the Job Future?

Radio and television broadcasting are two very popular careers of today. The professional-level jobs are very competitive, and thousands of liberal arts graduates apply for the few jobs available every spring. The small local stations are the least competitive and offer the beginner the most valuable diverse experience in communications. The chances for jobs are best with radio because there are many more of them and they hire more beginners.

RELATED CAREERS

commercial and public radio
commercial and public television
cable television

WHERE CAN I GET MORE INFORMATION?

Professional group
National Association of Broadcasters
1771 North Street, NW
Washington, D.C. 20036

Trade journals
Broadcasting
1735 Descales Street, NW
Washington, D.C. 20036

CableVision
Titsch Publishing, Inc.
1130 Delaware Plaza, P.O. Box 4305
Denver, CO 80204

RADIO BROADCASTING

WRITER

Writes clear and meaningful copy for newspapers, magazines, books, technical and trade brochures, and advertising.

What's It Like to Be a Writer?

A newspaper editor for a small city paper processes copy, writes stories, puts on headlines, marks pictures, dummies pages, checks teletype setters and composition, opens stacks of mail, and answers the phone, which rings constantly. A daily newspaper has a fast pace and a deadline atmosphere not found in other writing jobs. Beginning reporters are assigned civic, club, and police-court proceedings. As they gain experience, they may report more important events. Reporters may advance to reporting for larger papers or press services. Magazine writers write features or are magazine researchers, interviewers, and co-writers. Magazine production is similar to newspaper production in that both are dependent upon advertising for profits. The magazine personnel work closely with their advertising agency. The pace on a magazine is faster than in book publishing because magazine personnel have weekly or monthly deadlines. Fashion writers write about fashion for department store ads, trade publications, advertising agencies, and newspaper columns. Radio and TV news writers put the news into short sentences for listening purposes rather than reading purposes on news programs. The major networks have a staff of writers for their newscasters. Technical writers rewrite technical and scientific articles for use by nontechnical people or people in other scientific fields. Andrew Potok, author of the poignant book *Ordinary Daylight: Portrait of an Artist Going Blind,* says, "What I like best about writing is what I liked best about painting. The opportunity to sit and think and spin tales. It's an incredible privilege to lock yourself up in a room and plumb the depths to spin those tales. That's not to say it's easy and goes well. Like psychoanalysis, it's terribly difficult, as self-discipline and interior work always are. But still, I am always awed by the privilege I have of spending my life writing."

What Education and Skills Will I Need?

High school: Preparation for college, with as much language skill and experience as you can get. Any part-time or summer work on a local newspaper will help you find out what some writing jobs are like. Work on as many school publications as you can while in high school.

College: Writers come from journalism, English, and liberal arts majors, and from a great variety of programs. Most commercial writers have a college degree; however, college is not a necessity to be a successful writer. Writing and communication skills, together with a special style and interesting experiences, are what counts.

Personal skills: Writing skills, imagination, curiosity, resourcefulness, an accurate memory, and ability to work alone or in a bustling environment are all necessary for most writing jobs.

How Many Writers Are There and Where Do They Work?

There are 57,000 reporters and correspondents for newspapers and other media. There are 20,000 technical writers in electronics and aerospace industries, and most are men. About 110,000 writers and editors work on books, magazines, journals, newsletters, radio, TV, and movies. Most of the book publishing jobs are in New York City, while newspaper jobs are in almost every medium-sized town in the U.S. where smaller and special-interest newspapers are flourishing.

$ $ $ $ $

In 1980, newspaper reporters who worked under union contracts started at $250 a week. Reporters with experience averaged $406 a week, and top reporters made $616. Beginning salaries for writers and editorial assistants ranged from $12,000 to $16,000 a year. Experienced editors made up to $31,000 a year, and top-level editors earned over $50,000 a year. Very few writers of books can make their living from their books.

What Is the Job Future?

The writing jobs in urban centers are glamorous and competitive. Other than for the technical writing jobs, thousands of English and journalism majors look for writing jobs each fall in

WRITER

New York and other major cities. Every bit of experience counts, and if you can publish while in college, or work in a writing job during the summers, you will have a head start on the competition. Best chances for newspapers are in smaller towns and with special-interest papers. Most technical writers enter the work after several years' experience in technology or engineering.

RELATED CAREERS

journalist
translator
copywriter
fiction writer
nonfiction writer
biographer
screen writer

WHERE CAN I GET MORE INFORMATION?

Professional groups

American Newspaper Publishers Association
Box 17407
Dulles International Airport
Washington, D.C. 20041

The American Society of Magazine Editors
575 Lexington Avenue
New York, NY 10022

Trade journals

Publishers Weekly
1180 Avenue of the Americas
New York, NY 10036

Editor and Publisher—The Fourth Estate
850 Third Avenue
New York, NY 10022

Journal of Technical Writing and Communications
Baywood Publishing Company
Farmingdale, NY 11735

EDUCATION

College Professor
College Student Personnel
Early Childhood Educator
Elementary School Teacher
High School Teacher
Librarian
Museum Personnel
Physical Education Teacher
School Administrator
School Counselor
Special Education Teacher

About these careers *There are 2.5 million teachers plus professors and librarians represented by the descriptions in this section, and all of them require a college education. Most of the jobs require a master's degree or a doctorate for professional certification or promotion.*

Education careers require more education for less pay and have the bleakest outlook for future jobs than any other cluster. The oversupply of teachers graduating each year from colleges, the decrease in funding for education, the numbers of experienced teachers being laid off and looking for other educational jobs, the declining birthrate and school enrollments, and the closing down of the Department of Education on the federal level make the field very competitive.

Every state offers an education major in its state college or university. Write to your own State Department of Education (in your state's capital) and inquire which schools offer this major. If you choose to go to a liberal arts college, there are several options for certification in elementary and secondary education, including: summer school, a master's degree program, and correspondence courses.

If you are still convinced that education is the field for you, your best bet is to specialize in inner-city teaching, vocational and technical education, bilingual education, math and science, or education for the disabled, gifted, or disadvantaged. The computer industry has been draining the education's supply of math teachers and therefore creating the biggest demand in public schools and colleges in the field of mathematics.

Physical science is the only field with teacher shortages and funds for jobs. Bilingual and special education have shortages, but local school districts have cut these budgets because of cuts in federal money.

COLLEGE PROFESSOR

Assists students in college-level learning and in credentialing.

What's It Like to Be a College Professor?

Roberto Chavez, a Texas professor married to a professor, writes that the lifestyle of two college professors can make a most interesting family life: "We take turns tending to our children and sharing the domestic work, as most of our career time is flexible and can be done at home. College professors who teach full-time average 8 to 12 hours a week in the classroom. Higher-ranking professors who advise graduate students and who are actively engaged in research may spend only 4 to 6 hours a week in actual classroom teaching. Outside the classroom, much of the time is spent in preparation for teaching, grading student work, and keeping up with the subject matter. Most professors do research and write for their professional journals. The summer vacation can be spent teaching in summer school, conducting a research project, or on vacation."

What Education and Skills Will I Need?

High school: Preparation for college, with as strong an academic program as you can handle well.

College: Preparation for graduate school in whatever major you show the most ability and interest. Your graduate work doesn't have to be in the same field as your undergraduate work, although it is usually related. As you learn more about your academic abilities and interest, your major field may change. Plan to get your Ph.D. if you want to be a college professor.

Personal skills: A professor needs to be curious about learning, and able to share his enthusiasm and interest in his subject with his students. He must like detail and be persistent, in order to follow through on academic research and writing.

How Many Professors Are There and Where Do They Work?

There are 691,000 college professors. Half of all college professors are employed in eight states, each with college enroll-

COLLEGE PROFESSOR

ments exceeding 2,000,000: California, Illinois, Massachusetts, Michigan, New York, Ohio, Pennsylvania, and Texas.

$ $ $ $ $

In 1980, the average salary for a nine-month contract for a college instructor was $15,179; for an assistant professor, $18,900; for an associate professor, $23,199; and for a full professor, $30,738. Beginning salaries are much less than the average.

What Is the Job Future?

College teaching opportunities will be very competitive through the 1980s, as college enrollments decline and the number of Ph.D.s increases. The most number of jobs will be in science and engineering for those with Ph.D. degrees. The overproduction of college professors in the last few years has resulted in decreased opportunities in most fields. The rapid growth of community colleges will provide some jobs, but the trend in higher education is toward continuing education for adults, who will attend college part-time.

RELATED CAREERS

college administrator
dean of students
college librarian
admissions officer
career counselor

WHERE CAN I GET MORE INFORMATION?

Professional group
American Association of University Professors
1 Dupont Circle, Suite 500
Washington, D.C. 20036

Trade journal
AAUP Bulletin
AAUP
1 Dupont Circle, Suite 500
Washington, D.C. 20036

COLLEGE STUDENT PERSONNEL

Helps students meet their personal, social, housing, and recreational needs.

What's It Like to Be a Director of Student Personnel?

The Director of Student Personnel, sometimes called Vice-president for Student Affairs, is responsible for individualizing education for the college students. He can be responsible for counseling students, advising student government officers, and for overseeing residence halls programs, orientation programs for new students, fraternities, student honoraries, and communications between faculty and students. All these activities become very meaningful when working with each student to try to enable them to take advantage of all the educational opportunities on campus. Marc Freidman, Director of Student Personnel in a northwest college of liberal arts, encourages people to go into college personnel if they like the college style of living, and if they have a commitment to education and students. Adult students have different concerns from younger students, often combining family life with student life and a job. College personnel have to catch up with these needs.

What Education and Skills Will I Need?

High school: Preparation for college, with a broad range of academic subjects.

College: Many students prepare for graduate school with a major in social sciences or education. A master's degree is required in student personnel in higher education, and a doctorate is required for the bigger universities and top career jobs.

Personal skills: The ability to work with people of all backgrounds and ages; emotional stability while under pressure from students, parents, and faculty; and patience when working with conflicting viewpoints are necessary skills in college personnel.

How Many College Personnel Workers Are There and Where Do They Work?

There are 50,000 college student personnel workers and two-thirds are men. The jobs they hold include dean of men, dean of students, director of admissions, residence hall dean, registrar, counselor, financial aid officer, foreign student advisor, student union worker, student government specialist, and activities director. Every two-year and four-year college in the country hires student personnel workers.

$ $ $ $ $

In 1981, the median salary of student personnel directors was $20,671 a year.

What Is the Job Future?

Competition for work is expected through the 1980s. The tight budgets of all higher education institutions has cut many jobs in personnel. The rise in the number of student services could mean more demand for specialized college personnel workers, but lower residential college enrollments and an increase in personnel job applicants will make jobs difficult to get.

RELATED CAREERS

high school counselor
industrial personnel manager
school administrator
school psychologist

WHERE CAN I GET MORE INFORMATION?

Professional group
American College Personnel Association
Two Skyline Place
5203 Leesburg Pike
Falls Church, VA 22041

Trade journal
Journal of College Student Personnel
Two Skyline Place
5203 Leesburg Pike
Falls Church, VA 22041

EARLY CHILDHOOD EDUCATOR

Teaches children from two through five years old; day-care workers also take responsibility for infants.

What's It Like to Be an Early Childhood Educator?

Working with small groups in an unstructured situation for a few hours a day is the usual preschool schedule. The program consists of reading to the children, painting, working with clay and crafts, free play, music, dance, teaching colors and numbers, and talking about systems of services and transportation and families. Day-care and child-care centers often run from 7:00 A.M. until 7:00 P.M., and children come and go according to the hours their parents work. As more two-career families send their preschool children to care centers, jobs will increase for professionals in this crucial program.

Kelvin Seifert, head teacher at the demonstration preschool at San Jose State University, writes that male teachers in a child-care center face special problems in what has been a female work situation. The children often mistrust a man in this role, and some other female teachers question a man's motivation for working in this career. According to Seifert, most male child-care workers work part-time and don't remain long in the field. Often, men get experience for an administrative job in child-care.

What Education and Skills Will I Need?

High school: Preparation for college.

College: You can prepare for early childhood education with a two-year program in a community college, or a degree program in a four-year college, or an advanced degree program. Most nursery schools are private, and a degree is not required for teaching. Many nursery schools are informal and are co-operatives involving parents of the children in the teaching and planning of the school. Day-care centers and government programs for early childhood education will increasingly require degrees; master's degrees will be necessary for administration of these programs.

Personal skills: Ability to be firmly low-keyed in order to allow children self-expression in a relaxed learning environment, an avid interest in growth and development of small children, and the ability to be relaxed in an active setting are needed for early childhood educators.

How Many Early Childhood Educators Are There and Where Do They Work?

There are 239,000 nursery school and kindergarten teachers, and very few are men. Most communities have several morning and afternoon nursery school sessions.

$ $ $ $ $

Salaries vary more than any other teaching job because a school may be in a parent's home and dependent upon how many children enroll. College graduates working in public and university nursery schools begin at about the same salary as elementary teachers do, around $10,000 a year.

What Is the Job Future?

Two-career families have created the need for more day care and early-childhood care for the children of working parents. The government has responded very slowly and often not at all on a federal level. However, as parents make this issue a priority, day care will be forthcoming for children from all economic levels. The programs will provide an increasing number of opportunities for qualified people to establish and run both part-time and full-time children's-care centers and early-education centers.

RELATED CAREERS

elementary school teacher
industrial training manager
salesperson

WHERE CAN I GET MORE INFORMATION?

Professional groups

National Association for the Education of Young Children
1834 Connecticut Avenue, NW
Washington, D.C. 20009

Association for Childhood Education International
3615 Wisconsin Avenue, NW
Washington, D.C. 20016

Trade journals

Day Care and Child Development Reports
Plus Publications
2814 Pennsylvania Avenue, NW
Washington, D.C. 20007

Young Children
1834 Connecticut Avenue, NW
Washington, D.C. 20009

ELEMENTARY SCHOOL TEACHER

Teaches science, mathematics, language, and social studies to children in kindergarten through sixth grade.

What's It Like to Be an Elementary School Teacher?

Robert Braun, with twenty years' experience in business and technology, shares a fifth-grade teaching job with his wife. He doesn't know of one male who has spent a lifetime in elementary teaching. "Most try it for a few years, go back to school for administration or guidance, or switch to business as their financial pressure mounts." Braun really likes the diversification of duties—opportunities for crafts, woodworking, and art teaching that go with his job. He doesn't like detailed record keeping, such as recording lunch money allocations. The Brauns are in an innovative job situation, sharing one job. They try to split their school duties equally, and try to apportion home chores equally, too. "However, a particular home duty usually ends up being done by the person who tolerates that work best." About a shared job, he says, "The basic choice is between enough time or enough money. Adequate free time, without sufficient funds to do the things you want in that time, is not always satisfactory. A commitment to doing with less is the only solution, and this is not always practical with young people. I have found it possible to do without things because for a time I had those things, and I am making a voluntary choice to change my life. I doubt if I could do this if I were twenty years younger, with small children to provide for. But then, I am convinced that things are changing."

What Education and Skills Will I Need?

High school: Preparation for college, with as broad a program as possible. Most elementary teachers teach all subjects, including music, arts, and physical education, so be prepared!

College: Four-year college with a major in elementary education is required. A teaching certificate is awarded by every state, and many states require a fifth year of preparation for a permanent certification. Plan your fifth year or master's degree in a special area of education, such as administration.

Personal skills: Dependability, good judgment, and enthusiasm for young children are needed.

How Many Elementary School Teachers Are There and Where Do They Work?

Of the 1.6 million elementary school teachers, 15 percent are men, with an additional 60,000 principals and supervisors who are mostly men. They teach elementary school in every city, town, and village in the United States.

$ $ $ $ $

Salaries are determined by level of education, work experience, and the particular town in which teachers are employed. Most states have a minimum of $10,000 for beginning teachers, and the average salary for all elementary teachers in 1980 was $16,879 for a ten-month contract.

What Is the Job Future?

Overcrowded! The decline in school enrollments of elementary students and the overproduction of teacher graduates have caused a very competitive situation for teaching jobs. Many graduates cannot find a teaching job. The best possibilities for jobs are in the inner city, rural areas, or in work with the disabled. Some predict the job market will improve with a higher birthrate in the 1980s.

RELATED CAREERS

administrator	public relations representative
training manager	salesperson

WHERE CAN I GET MORE INFORMATION?

Professional group
National Education Association
1201 16th Street, NW
Washington, D.C. 20036

Trade journal
Today's Education
National Education Association
1201 16th Street, NW
Washington, D.C. 20036

HIGH SCHOOL TEACHER

Teaches a specific subject in junior or senior high school, grades 7 through 12.

What's It Like to Be a High School Teacher?

High school teachers teach 4 or 5 classes a day and supervise study halls, lunch cafeteria, and extracurricular activities. As a student, you have a better idea of what a high school teacher does than any other career because you see them at work all of the time! You certainly notice which ones enjoy their work, which ones make the most sense to you. If you want a career like those of the teachers who are really reaching you, you have a good example before you of what their life is like.

John Slayton, a high school teacher abroad for the U.S. Department of Defense, has taught military dependents in Japan, Turkey, and Holland. He loves the lifestyle, has an apartment in the Dutch village nearby rather than on the military base where he teaches, and shares with other American teachers the advantages of living in a foreign country and of traveling. Slayton says the frustrating part of his work is not having a solution for the small group of students who are trapped in our educational system and who disrupt the learning process of their classmates. What he likes best is "the satisfaction of helping young people prepare for an independent, successful career in our increasingly complex world, as they respond to what they learn about themselves and the world. Teaching," continues Slayton, "is a daily challenge and a wonderful variety of experiences that the students continually offer."

What Education and Skills Will I Need?

High school: Preparation for college, with as broad a program as possible.

College: Major in the subject you wish to teach, or a related subject if you are planning to attend graduate school. Each state has its own certification system, and many require a master's degree for permanent certification. There are many ways for you to do graduate work, including summer school, evening school, and correspondence courses.

Personal skills: Good teachers have a desire to work with young people, an interest in a special subject, and the ability to motivate others and to relate knowledge to them.

How Many High School Teachers Are There and Where Do They Work?

There are 1.2 million secondary school teachers and half of them are men, although most high school administrators and supervisors are men. Teachers teach in every community in the country, a big advantage for a person who wants a job that is available anywhere.

$ $ $ $ $

Salaries vary with each community, educational background, and experience. In 1980, the average salary for a high school teacher was $17,725 a year. Most states now have a minimum salary of $10,000 for a beginner with a bachelor's degree.

What Is the Job Future?

The U.S. is oversupplied with high school teachers and will be through the 1980s. The best chances for getting a job are in mathematics, natural sciences, and physical sciences.

RELATED CAREERS

administrator
training manager
public relations representative
salesperson

WHERE CAN I GET MORE INFORMATION?

Professional group
National Education Association
1201 16th Street, NW
Washington, D.C. 20036

Trade journal
Today's Education
National Education Association
1201 16th Street, NW
Washington, D.C. 20036

LIBRARIAN

Selects and organizes collections of books and other media and provides people access to information.

What's It Like to Be a Librarian?

A librarian offers the services of getting books and other information to individuals and special groups, of educating the public about what is available, and of helping all ages to a wonderful world of books that so often gives new and first interests to readers. The computer revolution is introducing information and the processing of information at a rate beyond everyone's imagination. Nowadays, librarians must have computer science skills and a new awareness of the information explosion of the 1980s. In large libraries, many librarians specialize and have a single function, such as cataloging, publicity, reference work, or working with a special subject such as art, medicine, or science. *Public librarians* serve all kinds of readers; *school librarians* work only with the students and staff of their school; and *university librarians* work with students, staff, and research workers. LeRoy Marshall, Boston Public Library specialist in microfilms, likes the quiet, serious enjoyment people share when coming to the library. He gets a month's vacation a year and says then he enjoys the liveliness of his young family in contrast to the silence at work.

What Education and Skills Will I Need?

High school: Preparation for college, with as broad a program as possible. Verbal and language skills are important to develop.

College: Strong liberal arts program to prepare for a graduate degree in library science. A reading knowledge of one foreign language is often required, and computer science is increasingly more essential to the job.

Personal skills: Good librarians have an intellectual curiosity and an interest in helping others to use library materials.

How Many Librarians Are There and Where Do They Work?

There are 135,000 full-time professional librarians, and another 10,500 individuals work as audiovisual specialists in

General Industrial Education
Machine Tool Operation
MACHINE TOOL METALWORKING
UNDERSTANDING ELECTRICITY
Architecture: Drafting and Design
CAREER CORE COMPETENCIES

LIBRARIAN

school media centers. Five percent are men. In addition, there are many part-time and nongraduate-degree librarians working in the public libraries all over the country. More than half of the professional librarians are public school librarians, one-fourth are public librarians, and one-fifth are college or university librarians.

$ $ $ $ $

In 1980, a graduate school librarian started at $13,127 a year. In private industry, beginning technical librarians averaged $14,500 a year, and those with five years' experience averaged $21,300 a year. Most school librarians are paid according to the regular teachers' scales of their individual schools.

What Is the Job Future?

The large number of library school graduates and the declining school population make it a competitive field. Information management outside the library setting is expected to offer excellent opportunities for library school graduates.

RELATED CAREERS

archivist
museum curator
publisher's representative
information scientist
book critic

WHERE CAN I GET MORE INFORMATION?

Professional groups

American Library Association
50 East Huron Street
Chicago, IL 60611

Special Libraries Association
235 Park Avenue South
New York, NY 10003

Trade journal

Top of the News
50 East Huron Street
Chicago, IL 60611

MUSEUM PERSONNEL

Creates museum exhibits and manages the work of an art museum, a natural history museum, or an historical or industrial museum.

What's It Like to Be in Museum Personnel?

Directors and curators of a museum design and install exhibits, organize demonstrations, acquire new art objects for the collections, revise old exhibits, and prepare budgets for the programs. Assistants to the curators take care of the slide collections, give evening lectures, take museum slides to schools for presentations, help in library research work, and help curators install new exhibits. Bill Waltham, an art history graduate student, works in the National Gallery in Washington, D.C., during his summer vacations. He feels that experience is absolutely necessary for a job when he graduates because of the tight competition for museum jobs. Waltham says, "Every art history major I know wants to work in a museum. You have to do something unique to have a chance for these few jobs, especially with federal, state, and municipal budgets cut to bare bone in the arts."

What Education and Skills Will I Need?

High school: Preparation for college, with emphasis on art and social sciences.

College: Most people in museum personnel are art history or anthropology graduates. Graduate degrees in museum careers are given in a few universities.

Personal skills: Creativity, an interest in history and art, and the ability to teach others is needed to be happy in museum work.

How Many Museum Workers Are There and Where Do They Work?

Fewer men than women work in museums, and the pay is very low for the level of education required and amount of responsibility involved. Most curators work in the major cities where the large museums are—New York, Chicago, Los Angeles, and Boston.

$ $ $ $ $

In 1980, college graduates started at $12,000 to $14,000 a year, with small advances coming very infrequently.

What Is the Job Future?

Beginning jobs for college graduates are very competitive in spite of the low pay. Art history graduates love their work in the museums, and thousands apply each spring to the museums all over the country for the few openings. An advanced degree is the best chance for a beginning job.

RELATED CAREERS

librarian
anthropologist
art designer

WHERE CAN I GET MORE INFORMATION?

Professional group
American Association of Museums
2233 Wisconsin Avenue, NW
Washington, D.C. 20007

Trade journal
Museum News
American Association of Museums
2233 Wisconsin Avenue, NW
Washington, D.C. 20007

PHYSICAL EDUCATION TEACHER

Teaches physical education and health to students from kindergarten through college.

What's It Like to Be a Physical Education Teacher?

The physical education teacher teaches students an activity in an informal setting within the school system. He is often tuned in to the students, their needs, problems, and the development of their lives. Teaching any subject can be helpful to the students, but the physical education teacher is often called upon to help other staff members, the guidance department, and the administration to know more about the behavior of a student. The physical education teacher gets to know his students well because sports and after-school activities offer a different type of learning situation. The teacher usually plans his own physical education program, with an emphasis on the sports and activities in which he is interested, the community in which he teaches, and the facilities available.

Roberto Mantilla, a Texas high school teacher, adds, "Broader programs to include individual sports away from school, such as weekend skiing, cross-country skiing, biking, and backpacking as part of the physical education program, is the developmental trend in programs." Dr. N. M. Shepard, Professor of Physical Education in Ohio, reminds young men that "this is not for you if you just live to play sports. It is an educational career, and sports are the medium for teaching students. Sports are one place where students can learn about leadership, aggression, and competition with everyone's approval."

What Education and Skills Will I Need?

High school: Preparation for college, with an emphasis on science and mathematics. Participate in as many sports as possible.

College: Major or minor in physical education. A master's degree is needed for certification in many states, and always for college teaching. Anatomy, physiology, and health courses are

PHYSICAL EDUCATION TEACHER

required for a physical education major. Mantilla advises students to work summers in recreation programs to get the edge on experience.

Personal skills: Physical education teachers must be athletic, have an ability to encourage those who are not athletic, an interest in total development of children, a sense of fairness, and an ability to encourage youth toward good health.

How Many Physical Education Teachers Are There and Where Do They Work?

Every high school and most elementary schools have a physical education teacher. Summer recreational and administrative work is always available with camps and playgrounds.

$ $ $ $ $

Salaries are the same as those of all other teachers within a particular school system. In 1981, most high school teachers averaged $17,725 a year.

What Is the Job Future?

As in other teaching jobs, there are more teachers than jobs now and through the 1980s. The best chances will be in special schools, inner-city schools, and rural schools.

RELATED CAREERS

teacher	athletic director
coach	athletic trainer

WHERE CAN I GET MORE INFORMATION?

Professional group
American Association of Health, Physical Education, and Recreation (AAHPER)
1201 16th Street, NW
Washington, D.C. 20036

Trade journal
Scholastic Coach
50 West 44 Street
New York, NY 10036

SCHOOL ADMINISTRATOR

Manages, directs, and coordinates the activities of a school, college, or university.

What's It Like to Be an Assistant School Superintendent?

"The first couple of hours each day are hectic but routine," says Assistant Superintendent Lawrence LeCours, "and involve responding to school bus problems, maintenance problems such as lack of heat in a section of one of the schools, or setting up meetings with teachers. Lunch varies from a ten-minute bite at the desk to eating in the school cafeteria with other school personnel or in a local restaurant with town officials. No day is the same, with meetings with principals and teachers to discuss curriculum and changes in the program. The day usually ends at 5 P.M. or 6 P.M. But about three evenings a week, it continues with meetings from 10 P.M. until midnight. The evening sessions are crucial for they are the part of the job that determines, in great measure, what will occur in the school programs. Administration is not for the clock watchers—a spouse or friends that have their own life interests and time commitments are a must. It's an exciting and challenging career, especially when you realize you are dealing with the leaders of tomorrow." Husband and father of two young children, LeCours says what he likes least about the job is the evening time away from his family. What he likes most is the many people he meets and the knowledge that what he does and believes has an influence on the children's educational process.

What Education and Skills Will I Need?

High school: Preparation for any college major that relates to teaching or education.

College: Major in any subject you wish to teach in school or college. If you want to be a college dean, college president, or superintendent of a large-city high school, prepare for a master's degree and work toward your doctorate in administration.

Personal skills: An interest in the development of children, business abilities, and the ability to communicate with many diverse ideas and people are necessary.

How Many School Administrators Are There and Where Do They Work?

Every school system and college in the country have administrators. Of the more than one million teachers in secondary schools, there are 127,000 secondary principals and assistants. There are 23,640 superintendents and almost all of them are men.

$ $ $ $ $

Administrators usually get paid some percentage more than what the teachers earn in any school. A superintendent of a small school system, with a master's degree, earns about $20,000 a year, and a superintendent of a large school system, with a doctorate, earns $45,000 a year and more. In 1981, an elementary school principal averaged $27,923 a year, and a high school principal averaged $32,231 a year.

What Is the Job Future?

The employment outlook is competitive through the 1980s for administrators as it is for all educators. As the birthrate rises, the need for elementary school administrators may increase in the late 1980s.

RELATED CAREERS

teacher
management career in government or business

WHERE CAN I GET MORE INFORMATION?

Professional group
National Education Association
1201 16th Street, NW
Washington, D.C. 20036

Trade journal
Nation's Schools
McGraw-Hill Publications Company
230 West Monroe
Chicago, IL 60606

SCHOOL COUNSELOR

Helps students understand their interests, abilities, and personality characteristics better, in the context of their educational development.

What's It Like to Be a School Counselor?

Armendo Mendoza, a school counselor in southern California, says, "A school counselor brings students, parents, teachers, and community agency people together to help kids with their educational and career decision making. I help students evaluate themselves by explaining their test scores, marks, and teachers' reports with them." Besides a lot of paperwork with student records and college and job recommendations, the work also involves getting information to students about which courses to take, which schools to apply to, and which careers sound right for each student. Divorced with three high school students of his own, Mendoza tries to keep in touch with his children's concerns in order to better understand the teenagers he deals with at work. "Remarriages, new babies, and many names in each family all add up to more stress on everyone," explains Mendoza.

What Education and Skills Will I Need?

High school: Preparation for college. Most counselors teach a subject before going into guidance.

College: A master's degree in guidance and one to five years of teaching are required by most states to be a certified counselor. A doctorate is required for big-city administration careers in guidance.

Personal skills: Successful counselors have an interest in helping others take responsibility for themselves and an interest in working with other educators, parents, and teachers, who may have varying opinions about students' development.

How Many Counselors Are There and Where Do They Work?

There are 53,000 full-time school counselors and most work in the public secondary schools.

$ $ $ $ $

Salaries vary with the school system, but usually school counselors are paid more than classroom teachers, but not as much as administrators. In 1981, the average salary for a counselor with a master's degree was $20,600 a year. Experienced counselors in the major suburbs earn about $26,000 a year and often work eleven months a year.

What Is the Job Future?

The future is bleak through the 1980s. The decline in school population and the cuts in public school budgets are making guidance jobs very competitive.

RELATED CAREERS

psychologist	parole officer
social worker	rehabilitation counselor

WHERE CAN I GET MORE INFORMATION?

Professional group
American School Counselor Association
Two Skyline Place, Suite 400
5203 Leesburg Pike
Falls Church, VA 22041

Trade journal
Guidepost
American School Counselor Association
Two Skyline Place, Suite 400
5203 Leesburg Pike
Falls Church, VA 22041

SPECIAL EDUCATION TEACHER

Teaches children with disabilities who are unable to learn in large classrooms without special related services some of the time; or teaches children who learn best when they are separated into small groups all of the time.

What's It Like to Be a Special Education Teacher?

A special education teacher spends his day assessing students who have been referred for special education by classroom teachers, instructing children with disabilities in small groups, tutoring some children on a one-to-one basis, and supervising teachers' aides. He spends a lot of time consulting with classroom teachers about the students who leave their classrooms for tutoring but return to class and are "mainstreamed" most of the school day. A special education teacher also evaluates testing and is a regular team member for developing the Individualized Educational Program (IEP) for children with disabilities. Pete Sinot, a special education teacher in Minnesota who has a mentally retarded child of his own, says, "Once I learned to expect small accomplishments from the children, to slow down and let the activities of the day go at a natural pace for the children, I was fine. Until then, I was uptight about achievement, which caused anxiety and strife in the classroom." Sinot finds his work very rewarding. He tells us that he can really become involved in a student's life. He has learned to give what the student needs, rather than what he thinks the student needs.

What Education and Skills Will I Need?

High school: Preparation for college, with an emphasis on subjects that interest you.

College: Major in any subject, or in education, elementary education, or special education, and prepare for a master's degree. Most states require a master's degree for certification, although you can begin teaching with a bachelor's degree.

Personal skills: Patience with slow progress, the ability to work with disabled children and their parents, and the ability to see accomplishment in things that might seem small compared to the rest of the world.

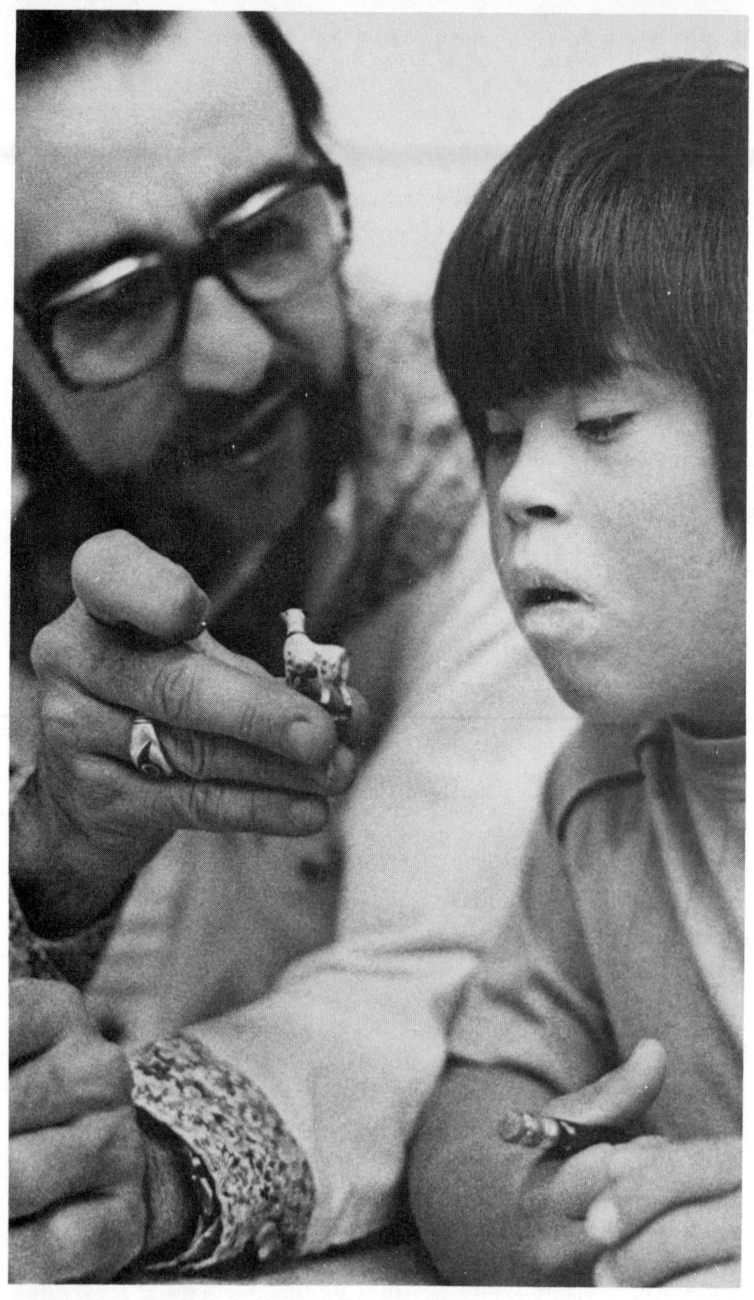

SPECIAL EDUCATION TEACHER

$ $ $ $ $

Salaries vary with the community and the school system. They are the same as other teachers' salaries within the school system, averaging $17,725 a year with experience.

What Is the Job Future?

The good opportunities for special education teachers of the 1970s have been drastically changed because the federal government has decreased funds in education, and local schools often consider this area an "extra."

RELATED CAREERS

rehabilitation counselor
occupational therapist
social worker
reading specialist

WHERE CAN I GET MORE INFORMATION?

Professional group
National Education Association
1201 16th Street, NW
Washington, D.C. 20036

Trade journal
Teaching Exceptional Children
Council for Exceptional Children
1411 South Jefferson Davis Highway, Suite 900
Arlington, VA 22202

GOVERNMENT

City Manager
Community Planner
Foreign Service Officer
Civil Service
Health and Regulatory Inspector
Law Enforcement
Lawyer
Military Careers
Peace Corps Volunteer

About these careers *Until very recently, the U.S. Government was the nation's largest employer. There are 14.5 million civilian workers in local, state, and federal government jobs. One out of every six employed persons in our country works in government. One-third of all government workers, or 4.6 million, are college graduates. In addition, there are 2.2 million military men and women on active duty.*

Although government employment has been a major career for college graduates in the past, job opportunities in government will be declining rapidly through 1990. If there are jobs, they are projected to occur in state and local agencies, who are getting more government responsibilities back from the federal government.

Preparing for a career with the government is different from preparing for most career clusters, because the government hires about every kind of career described in this book. Therefore, accountants, physicians, teachers, nurses, and purchasing agents are all careers that can be government careers. They require a great variety of educational backgrounds.

The government-related careers described in this cluster, such as city manager, community planner, and lawyer, require graduate work. For example, a master's degree, generally in public or business administration, is becoming increasingly important for those seeking a career in city management.

Volunteer jobs in the Peace Corps are limited to two years and do not necessarily lead to paying jobs that are directly related to that experience.

Beginning lawyers engaged in legal-aid work usually receive the lowest starting salaries. New lawyers starting their own practice may earn little more than expenses during the first few years. When a case is being tried, lawyers often work long hours and are under considerable pressure. In addition, they must keep up with the latest laws and court decisions. However, since lawyers in private practice can determine their own hours and workload, many stay in practice well past the usual retirement age.

People who work for the government find maximum security in terms of regular pay, regular work, vacations, a good retirement plan, and excellent health insurance.

CITY MANAGER

Administers and coordinates the day-to-day operations of the city.

What's It Like to Be a City Manager?

Planning for future growth, air and water pollution, and rising crime rates demand the services of a good city manager. He also is responsible for tax collection, law enforcement, public works, and preparing the budget. A city manager is responsible to the community's elected officials who hire him. In addition to daily activities of the city, he studies long-range problems of traffic, housing, crime, and urban renewal, and reports his findings to the elected council. He often works with citizens' groups and provides special reports to special meetings. Many of the citizens' group meetings are held at night, after a full work day.

What Education and Skills Will I Need?

High school: Preparation for college, with as much group experience in as many school activities as interest you.

College: A master's degree in public or municipal administration is necessary for the better jobs. Undergraduate work can be in business, engineering, recreation, or political science.

Personal skills: Ability to quickly isolate problems, identify their causes, and find solutions; good judgment; self-confidence; and the ability to work well with others are skills needed for this job.

How Many City Managers Are There and Where Do They Work?

There are 3,300 managers plus many more assistant managers and department heads in a city. This is a new and growing career. Over three-quarters of the city managers work for small cities with less than 25,000 population.

$ $ $ $ $

In 1980, new graduates started at $18,000 a year as assistant managers. Average salary for experienced managers was

$33,000 a year, ranging from $28,000 in small cities to $70,000 in cities with populations of 500,000 to one million.

What Is the Job Future?

Jobs will be competitive through the 1980s because there are many more graduates than jobs. Best opportunities are in the South and the West.

RELATED CAREERS

business administrator
hospital administrator
school administrator
airport manager

WHERE CAN I GET MORE INFORMATION?

Professional group
International City Management Association
1140 Connecticut Avenue, NW
Washington, D.C. 20036

Trade journal
Nation's Cities
National League of Cities
1612 K Street, NW
Washington, D.C. 20006

COMMUNITY PLANNER

Develops plans and programs for orderly growth and improvement of urban and rural communities.

What's It Like to Be a Community Planner?

Alfred Lima has a college degree in landscape architecture and a master's degree in community planning. He started his own planning firm in Boston and spends a lot of time getting projects for his firm. Right now, his biggest project is one with the federal government—fire prevention in urban areas. Lima likes being his own boss and doing something useful and creative like preserving the urban environment. The usual work includes master plans of the city, review of work completed by other staff members, and reading of professional journals and publications. In addition, he works on basic studies (such as data collection, economic base and regional analysis, population studies, map preparation); plans recommendations such as land-use allocation, utilities, municipal facilities, housing, open spaces, and recreation and beautification programs; and plans implementation such as budget, subdivision regulations, and citizen information programs. Lima is a new stepfather to three young children but still must plan on several evenings a week devoted to meetings with planning boards, civic groups concerned with planning, and professional meetings. He suggests that students learn the practical skills of graphics, drafting, and writing so they can do everything they need to run a business.

What Education and Skills Will I Need?

High school: Preparation for college, with an emphasis on mathematics, computer science, and social sciences.

College: A beginning job requires a master's degree in urban or regional planning, which is offered in 70 colleges and universities. To prepare for graduate school, major in architecture, engineering, economics, social science, or public administration.

Personal skills: Ability to think in spatial relationships and to visualize plans and designs, flexibility in solving problems, and ability to cooperate with others who have different ideas are necessary qualities for planners.

How Many Community Planners Are There and Where Do They Work?

Of the 23,000 city planners, 90 percent are men. The majority of planners work for the government in agencies such as city, county, or urban regional planning organizations. In addition to their regular job, many planners do part-time consulting work with a firm or private developer.

COMMUNITY PLANNER

$ $ $ $ $

In 1981, the beginning salary for a planner, with a master's degree, working with the federal government was $18,600 a year. Consultants are paid on a fee basis, which is based on their regional or national reputation. Directors of planning earn an average salary of $27,000 a year.

What Is the Job Future?

The employment outlook will become more competitive through the 1980s. Cuts in government spending and more graduates than jobs will limit the job opportunities drastically. Geographic mobility and willingness to work in small towns are important for many job seekers.

RELATED CAREERS

- planning engineer
- city manager
- architect

WHERE CAN I GET MORE INFORMATION?

Professional group
American Planning Association
1776 Massachusetts Avenue, NW
Washington, D.C. 20036

Trade journal
City
National Urban Coalition
2100 M Street, NW
Washington, D.C. 20037

FOREIGN SERVICE OFFICER

Serves in the overseas arm of the United States' foreign relations activities.

What's It Like to Be a Foreign Service Officer?

A foreign service officer protects and promotes the welfare and interest of the United States and the American people abroad. He works in the Department of State, which is responsible for advising the President on matters of foreign policy; conducting relations with foreign nations; protecting U.S. political, economic, and commercial interests overseas; and offering services to Americans abroad and to foreign nationals traveling to the United States. Henry Preston, a college graduate in history, with a master's in international relations and a Ph.D. from Yale University in Russian studies, says that he just passed the written and oral foreign service exams and is now looking into the duties and responsibilities of the four broad functions of the Department of State: administrative affairs, consular affairs, economic/commercial affairs, and political affairs. Preston will be given his first assignment within three months, but he gets to choose in which major function he wants to develop his career. The Department of State will decide where he and his family (pregnant wife and three-year-old son) will go, and how long they will stay. The whole family was interviewed before Preston was accepted into foreign service.

What Education and Skills Will I Need?

High school: Preparation for college, with emphasis in social sciences, history, government, and foreign language.

College: Foreign service officers come from liberal arts colleges with majors in English, foreign language, international relations, history, government, and a great variety of other fields. A master's degree is not a requirement, but most officers do have an advanced degree. Everyone applying for an appointment must take the written examination, which is given once each year, in December, in about 150 cities. Applications must be made by late October.

Personal skills: In addition to the ability to study and solve problems, representatives of the U.S. government must have a good physical appearance, be tactful, and have a pleasant personality.

How Many Foreign Service Officers Are There and Where Do They Work?

Some 3,400 foreign service officers serve as administrative, consular, economic, and political officers in more than 230 United States embassies and consulates in over 140 nations.

$ $ $ $ $

In 1980, beginning salaries ranged from $17,000 to $25,000 a year. The top salary is the same for all federal employees and is $52,750. In addition to salary, there are many fringe, living, and travel benefits.

What Is the Job Future?

Very competitive, since only 200 foreign service officers are appointed a year and thousands of qualified young people apply for the jobs.

RELATED CAREERS

international business sales
federal government career
import business manager

WHERE CAN I GET MORE INFORMATION?

Professional groups
Board of Examiners for the Foreign Service
Box 9317, Rosslyn Station
Arlington, VA 22209

Foreign Service Careers
U.S. Department of State
Washington, D.C. 20520

CIVIL SERVICE

Federal government jobs represent every kind of job found in private employment.

What's It Like to Be in Civil Service?

College graduates can enter career management, administrative and personnel management, and technical and professional jobs with the government. Two-year college graduates can enter technical assistance careers in economics, administration, writing, data processing, finance, accounting, law, library science, and physical science.

There are two ways to get a federal job. The first and most common is by taking the civil service examination and being placed on a civil service register. Whenever a job opening occurs in a federal agency, the registers are scanned and the names of the best-qualified applicants are sent to the agency. You can increase your chances of getting a federal job by filing in more than one category and by agreeing to move anywhere in the country. The advantage for men is the veteran's preference policy.

The second way to get a federal job is by political appointment. By law, there are over 3,000 high-level jobs that are filled in this way. If you are well known in your field, get in touch with your senator for a recommendation, or with your company for the President's Program for Executive Exchange. If you have not yet made a name for yourself in your career, you can work long and hard on a successful presidential campaign.

A short-term government service can offer you a valuable step up in your career. Carla A. Hills, former Secretary of the Department of Housing and Urban Development, says this about a government term, "As you gather experiences, including government experience, you become better at everything you do. It is the breadth of exposure that makes you valuable to an employer. In my view, government is incredibly stimulating, challenging, and broader than most people in the private sector believe. Your responsibilities invariably are greater than your job description." After three years of work in government service, the civil worker has career status. For example, if a parent leaves his job to raise children, he can return to the same job level rather than competing again for the level he left.

What Education and Skills Will I Need?

High school: Preparation for community college, business college, health training, or four-year college in any field that interests you.

College: The more education you have, the higher the career level open to you. Two-year college graduates take the Junior Federal Assistant Examination or the Junior Engineer and Science Assistant Examination to qualify for jobs. Four-year college graduates take the Federal Service Entrance Examination to qualify for trainee-level positions for careers.

Personal skills: Skills needed vary according to the career you select.

How Many Civil Service Workers Are There and Where Do They Work?

Each year, ten thousand federal jobs requiring college degrees are appointed and two-thirds of them go to men. In 1981, the federal government employed nearly 2 million white-collar workers. About 150,000 of them work in engineering, 150,000 in accounting, 120,000 in health service, and 45,000 in biological and agricultural science. One in eight federal employees works in Washington, D.C.; the remainder work all over the U.S. and abroad.

$ $ $ $ $

Salaries are paid according to the General Schedule (GS) and are set by Congress. The pay scale is set for all government employees in the professions, administrative jobs, and technical and clerical jobs. There are raises within each grade and increases are periodic for each grade. In 1981, graduates of a two-year college without experience started at $12,300 a year; graduates of a four-year college started at $15,900 or $17,700 a year; a person with a master's degree began work at $18,600 a year.

What Is the Job Future?

In the late 1970s, government service employed over 14.5 million workers. That means that one out of six employed persons in the U.S. worked for the government! The political trend is to heavily reduce federal employees, which is resulting in a rapid decline of federal jobs. No new jobs are being opened, and thousands of federal employees are job-hunting, causing a very competitive situation.

RELATED CAREERS

state government	post office
local government	military careers

WHERE CAN I GET MORE INFORMATION?

Professional group
U.S. Civil Service Commission
Washington, D.C. 20415

Trade journal
Civil Service Journal
Government Printing Office
Washington, D.C. 20402

HEALTH AND REGULATORY INSPECTOR

Checks compliance with federal health, safety, trade, and employment laws.

What's It Like to Be a Health and Regulatory Inspector?

A health and regulatory inspector holds a great variety of jobs, such as food and drug inspector, meat and poultry inspector, agriculture quarantine inspector, sanitarian, commodity grader, immigration inspector, customs inspector, aviation safety officer, mine inspector, wage-hour compliance officer, and alcohol, tobacco, and firearms inspector. Robert O'Connor, U.S. Customs Officer on the Vermont-Canadian border, says he likes the diversity of his work on a busy highway border. "We enforce the laws of every executive office—commerce, internal revenue, agriculture, etc. At a borderport, you must be accurate, because decisions are made immediately and can't be reviewed later. The worst part of the job is the negative confrontations with the public and the shifts necessary to cover twenty-four hours of work. It's hard on family life, but the work is usually rewarding because the American public is being protected through customs inspection."

What Education and Skills Will I Need?

High school: Preparation for community college or four-year college.

College: Most inspectors have two to four years of college, plus specialized work experience in the job they seek.

Personal skills: Inspectors must be responsible, good at detailed work, neat, and have good speaking and writing skills.

How Many Health and Regulatory Inspectors Are There and Where Do They Work?

There are over 112,000 inspection officers and 90 percent of them are men. Most work for federal government agencies, but others work for state governments.

$ $ $ $ $

In 1981, aviation and mining inspectors started at $18,585 a year. Other health and regulatory inspectors and graders started at $12,266 a year. Experienced immigration and customs inspectors averaged more than $20,000 a year.

What Is the Job Future?

Chances for jobs will be limited through the 1980s. Cuts in government employment and policy against government regulation will result in fewer jobs.

RELATED CAREERS

bank examiner
construction inspector
law enforcement

WHERE CAN I GET MORE INFORMATION?

Professional group
Interagency Board of U.S. Civil Service Examiners
1900 E Street, NW
Washington, D.C. 20415

Trade journal
American Industrial Hygiene Association Journal
35 New Street
Worcester, MA 01605

LAW ENFORCEMENT

Careers, such as police officer or special agent for the Federal Bureau of Investigation, designed to preserve law and order by investigating and apprehending law breakers.

What's It Like to Be in Law Enforcement?

FBI special agents investigate violations of federal laws, such as bank robberies, kidnapping, frauds and thefts against the government, espionage, and sabotage. Brian Hurley, a law school graduate, is a trainee at the FBI Academy at the U.S. Marine Corps Base in Quantico, Virginia. He is married, and he and his wife are expecting a baby. Hurley reminds us that the FBI is a fact-gathering agency, not a protection or police agency. A special agent spends most of his time collecting evidence in cases in which the United States is an interested party. He usually works alone on cases where he has specialized knowledge. For instance, accountants may investigate bank embezzlements.

Police officers patrol high-crime neighborhoods on an eight-hour shift, investigate complaints about disorderly people, break up unruly crowds, and fill out report forms covering each activity. One police officer said that police patrols are more a form of social work than a test of physical endurance. The work involves keeping calm, offering help, and knowing the other agencies in the community that can help people. In large police departments, officers are usually assigned to a specific type of police duty, such as patrol or traffic duty, accident prevention, communications systems, or criminal investigation.

LAW ENFORCEMENT

State police officers patrol our highways and enforce motor laws. They issue traffic tickets to violators, give first aid at traffic accidents, and write reports of accidents. In addition, they radio for help for motorists who are stranded on the highway.

What Education and Skills Will I Need?

High school: Educational requirements vary with the department and the job level. For police officer work and FBI work, prepare for college and play sports to train for the physical qualifications required.

College: Even though a college degree is not a requirement for police work, you will have a better chance with a degree to be accepted into training in big city police departments, and for promotions. To become a special agent of the FBI, a college degree in accounting or a law degree is no longer required. Special agents come from a great variety of college majors.

Personal skills: Honesty, good judgment, a sense of responsibility, physical stamina, emotional stability, and excellent hearing and vision are all necessary for a law enforcement career.

How Many Law Enforcement Workers Are There and Where Do They Work?

There are 8,000 FBI special agents and they work in the 58 field offices all over the U.S. There are 495,000 full-time police officers who have jobs in every community in the country. State police officers number 55,000.

$ $ $ $ $

In 1980, police officers started from $1,300 to $1,520 a month, depending on the size of the city and their experience. Beginning salaries for state police averaged $14,000 a year. Experienced state police made from $18,000 to $20,000 a year. In 1981, FBI special agents started at $20,467 a year.

What Is the Job Future?

In time of high unemployment, police work is difficult to get. But those with college training and some work experience will have the best chance. Minorities will also have a good chance for work. For years, they were not hired in law enforcement, and now the law says they must be represented on police forces. An FBI special agent is a glamorous job with many applicants for the work.

RELATED CAREERS

detective	border patrol agent
secret service agent	Internal Revenue Service agent

WHERE CAN I GET MORE INFORMATION?

Professional groups

Local and State Police Departments

Director, FBI
U.S. Dept. of Justice
Washington, D.C. 20535

U.S. Secret Service
Personnel Division, Room 912
1800 G Street, NW
Washington, D.C. 20226

Trade journal

National Sheriff
NSA
1250 Connecticut Avenue, NW
Washington, D.C. 20036

LAWYER

Connects the legal system with changing human needs.

What's It Like to Be a Lawyer?

Most lawyers, also called attorneys, work in general practice and handle all kinds of legal work for clients, such as property deeds, divorces, making wills, and settling estates. Others specialize in various areas of corporate, criminal, labor, patent, real estate, tax, and international law. Because there is an oversupply of law graduates, many lawyers have gone into careers outside of legal work. Professional government jobs, political jobs, civil rights, and the FBI as well as business and private industry attract law school graduates. Keeping the law responsive to human needs is the work of lawyers. As our laws grow more complex, the work of lawyers takes on more importance in their clients' lives. Our lives are affected in new ways as the legal system takes on regulatory tasks in areas such as transportation, energy conservation, consumer protection, and social welfare.

Bill McDermit, married to his law partner, says there are certain activities that most lawyers do. "The most fundamental activity is interpretation of the law. Whether representing the defendant in a divorce case or the suing party (plaintiff) in a law suit, the lawyer has to know the relevant laws and the facts in the case to determine how the law affects the facts. Based on this determination, the lawyer decides what action is in the best interest of his client. To interpret the law, lawyers do research. They must keep up with their field in both legal and nonlegal matters. For example, an attorney representing electronics manufacturers follows the electronic trade journals as well as the laws. Divorce lawyers read about the changing role of the family in modern society, the different acceptable living arrangements, and the great variety of living and loving together. Most lawyers consult with clients to determine the details of problems, to advise them of the law, and to suggest action that might be taken. Finally, most lawyers write reports or briefs, which must be communicated clearly. Working in our own practice," reports McDermit, "gives us the kind of work and lifestyle we want together. We will not have children until we get this practice going, and maybe not even then. We work hard, and when we're finished, we really love to take off and have our time for sports and sun with no other worries or commitments."

What Education and Skills Will I Need?

High school: Preparation for college, with as much liberal arts and verbal and language skills as possible.

College: Prelaw graduates go to one of the 156 approved

three-year law schools, then they must pass the bar examinations in the state in which they will practice. English, history, government, economics, philosophy, and social sciences are important in prelaw. An understanding of society and its institutions is required for law. About one-fifth of all law students are enrolled in part-time divisions, usually night school.

Personal skills: Responsibility, interest in people and ideas, debating and writing skills, and ability to build trust and confidence in others are needed to be a successful lawyer.

How Many Lawyers Are There and Where Do They Work?

There are over 425,000 lawyers and three out of four are in private practice. More than half of them are in business for themselves. In addition, 22,000 lawyers work for the federal government and another 32,000 work for state and local governments.

$ $ $ $ $

In 1980, the average beginning salary for a new graduate hired by a law firm was from $10,000 to $35,000 a year. In 1981, the federal government started law school graduates at $18,600 or $22,500 a year. The average salary of the most experienced lawyers in private industry in 1980 was over $60,000 a year.

What Is the Job Future?

Very competitive. Many more graduates than jobs are expected through the 1980s. Those who specialize in tax, patent, or admirality law will get the salaried jobs. Others will set up their own practice in smaller towns or work in related fields.

RELATED CAREERS

negotiator
judge
legislator
FBI special agent

WHERE CAN I GET MORE INFORMATION?

Professional group
The American Bar Association
1155 60th Street
Chicago, IL 60637

Trade journal
Trial
American Trial Lawyer's Association
20 Garden Street
Cambridge, MA 02138

MILITARY CAREERS

Members of the Army, Navy, Air Force, Coast Guard, and Marine Armed Forces.

What's It Like to Be in the Military?

In peace time, it's like getting paid for job training and work experience. There are over 200 job-training courses in the Army for technical, medical, communications, and electronics jobs that you can choose *before* you enter the service. The job you can choose depends upon your present level of education and achievement. Each service has its own jobs, its own job-training, and its own educational programs. Check with the Army, the Air Force, the Navy, the Coast Guard, and the Marine Corps for specific details. You can enlist in a variety of combinations of active and reserve duty. Active duty ranges from two to six years, with three-year and four-year enlistments most common.

What Education and Skills Will I Need?

High school: Required for enlisted personnel. Preparation for college in any major to qualify for the officers' training programs.

College: Your major in college qualifies you for the job you wish to select in the service. The military can use any and all types of skills and educational achievements.

Other qualifications: You must be between 18 years old and 27 years old, a United States citizen, and in good physical condition. There is no restriction on marital status, but you cannot have dependents under 18 at the time you enlist.

How Many Military Workers Are There and Where Do They Work?

There are 2.2 million people in the armed forces. The Army has 777,000; the Air Force 558,000; the Navy 527,000; the Marines 188,000; and the Coast Guard 39,000. They are stationed in the United States and abroad, mostly in Europe. In addition are another 2 million men and women in the reserve units.

$ $ $ $ $

In 1980, basic pay and allowances for food and quarters for an officer started at $15,644 a year. Also included are medical and dental benefits, thirty days paid vacation, and special discounts on food and travel.

What Is the Job Future?

Because the military is now a volunteer rather than a draft organization, the military makes its offers as attractive as it can to recruit the number of workers it needs. High unemployment and recession result in many more enlistments. Many young people are interested in military education and training, which will continue to be exceptionally good for learning a skill and getting paid for it. Peace time is a good time to find opportunities for work in the military. The more education you have before you go join the military, the higher the job level at which you will start in the service. The Reagan administration is threatening to reinstate the draft and has promised big defense spending, which will increase military opportunities.

WHERE CAN I GET MORE INFORMATION?

Professional group

Write to or visit your local recruiting station for the latest official information. Look in your phone book, or write to the U.S. Army Recruiting Command, Fort Sheridan, IL 60037. When you are selecting your college, ask about ROTC programs. There are 500 Army, Navy, Marine, and Air Force units in college.

Trade journal
Army Times, Air Force Times, Navy Times,
Marine Corps, Coast Guard
Army Times Publishing Co.
475 School Street, SW
Washington, D.C. 20024

PEACE CORPS VOLUNTEER

Promotes world peace and friendship by providing trained humanpower, creating a better understanding of American people to others, and creating a better understanding of other peoples to Americans.

What's It Like to Be a Peace Corps Volunteer?

Peace Corps volunteers do any kind of job the developing country requests, although most teach or work in health or agriculture. Ricardo Campbell, a volunteer in São Mateus, Brazil, says there are many reasons for working for two years of your life in the Peace Corps, but a common theme is "the willingness to serve, to step beyond ourselves and our immediate comfort to help, in some small way, other people to help themselves." The daily living of the Peace Corps Volunteer (PCV) is spent eating the same food and living in the same lifestyle as the people who invited them.

What Education and Skills Will I Need?

High school: Preparation for college. Any skill or professional achievement can be used in the Peace Corps.

College: Ninety-six percent of the volunteers have attended college and most are liberal arts graduates. The Peace Corps is a temporary career or work experience, and many volunteers return home to go to graduate school. A thirteen-week training program is required before leaving the country.

How Many Peace Corps Volunteers Are There and Where Do They Work?

There are 5,400 volunteers in the Peace Corps serving two-year terms at a time. About 40 percent are teachers, 25 percent work in health nutrition and water supply, and 18 percent work in food production. Most are college graduates and 20 percent are married (and some have children). They are sent to the 60 countries who have invited them. Over half of the volunteers are 23 to 25 years old, 24 percent are 26 to 28 years old, and 8 percent are over 36 years old. Odlin Long, 79, has been in and out of the Peace Corps for twelve years in construction work. He is currently in Africa but has served in many other countries as well. Peace Corps volunteers serve in Africa, Latin America, North Africa, the Near East, South Asia, and the Pacific.

$ $ $ $ $

Travel and living allowance are paid, and the living allowance is based on the local conditions where the volunteer is working. In Ghana, volunteers earn $270 a month, more than most other countries because of the high cost of living. Most volunteers accumulate from $1,800 to $2,000 while in the Peace Corps. Many use some of this fund for extra traveling, before actually returning to the United States.

What Is the Job Future?

Even though the era of the Peace Corps has past, there will continue to be a need for volunteers of all ages. Peace Corps workers return from overseas with an interest in another area of the world. They have had the opportunity to learn and use a foreign language and to know the culture and traditions of the country in which they worked. Many of the volunteers return home to take advanced work in college. Of those who do not return to school, most enter public service. The following skills are needed and are scarce among applicants: diesel mechanics, forestry, nursing, math and science teachers, and engineers.

RELATED CAREERS

government service
missionary
international business

WHERE CAN I GET MORE INFORMATION?

Professional group
ACTION
806 Connecticut Avenue, NW
Washington, D.C. 20525
Call ACTION toll free at 800-424-8580.

HEALTH

ADMINISTRATOR

Health Service Administrator
Medical Records Administrator

PRACTITIONER

Chiropractor
Dental Hygienist
Dentist
Doctor
Nurse
Optometrist
Osteopathic Physician
Podiatrist
Veterinarian

THERAPIST

Occupational Therapist
Physical Therapist
Speech and Hearing Therapist

OTHER

Dietitian
Medical Technologist
Pharmacist

About these careers *There are almost 4 million people working in health-related jobs. Today, there are an estimated 200 to 400 individual health-care careers, and the options within each profession have never been greater. Besides doctors, nurses, dentists, and therapists, other careers are the behind-the-scenes technologists, technicians, administrators, and assistants. Registered nurses, physicians, pharmacists, and dentists make up the largest professional health occupations. Nearly 2 million health jobs are represented in this career cluster.*

Hospitals employ about half of all workers in the health field. Others work in clinics, private practice, laboratories, pharmacies, public health agencies, and mental health centers.

Most of the jobs described here require a number of years of preprofessional and professional college work, and a passing grade on a state licensing examination. Only the jobs of dental hygienist and nurse require less than a four-year program to start in an entry-level position.

Working conditions usually involve long hours. Because health facilities such as nursing homes and hospitals operate around the clock, administrators in these institutions may be called at all hours to settle emergency problems. Also, some travel may be required to attend meetings or, in the case of state public health departments and voluntary health agency administrators, to inspect facilities in the field.

Most dental offices are open five days a week and some dentists have evening hours. Dentists usually work between 40 and 45 hours a week, although many spend more than 50 hours a week in the office with technical and business-related work.

Many physicians have long working days and irregular hours. Most specialists work less hours a week than general practitioners.

Veterinarians in rural areas may spend much time traveling to and from farms, and may have to work outdoors in any weather.

Nursing, one of the largest professional-level occupations, has an employment projection of 1.2 million by 1985. The demand for nurses will continue to provide an increasing number of jobs, giving nurses more negotiating power as they plan their time and tasks.

The demand for health care will increase as the population grows older and the public increasingly becomes health conscious. Expansion of coverage under prepayment medical programs that make it easier for persons to pay for hospitalization and medical care also contribute to growth in the health cluster. In addition to jobs created by employment growth, many new jobs will open as a result of turnover and retirement.

Where are there more people than jobs? Besides an oversupply of doctors in many parts of the country, there is an oversupply of people with a master's in public health and in hospital administration, and there are too many general medical technologists.

And where are the jobs? In all areas of nursing, nurse anesthetist in particular; in respiratory, occupational, and physical therapy; in nuclear medicine and radioisotopes; and in emergency room medical care.

HEALTH SERVICE ADMINISTRATOR

Plans programs, sets policies, and makes decisions for hospitals, medical clinics, nursing homes, and other health facilities.

What's It Like to Be a Health Service Administrator?

The work involves hiring and training personnel, preparing the budget, planning space needs, purchasing supplies and equipment, and arranging for laundry, mail, and telephone services for patients and staff. Health administrators work closely with the medical and nursing staff, and try to make all of the necessary personnel and equipment available to them. Joseph Maillaux, Assistant Health Administrator, is in his forties and father of four children. He finds the work very exciting. He is in a medical-school teaching hospital and likes the challenge of solving problems as they arise. For instance, when the power goes off in the operating room, he goes right to the scene in the power room with the engineers. "You must decide quickly what other power to shut off elsewhere in order to direct it to the operating room. You're paid to make good and fast decisions," says Maillaux. Executive Vice-president Edward H. Noroian, of the Presbyterian Hospital of New York City, agrees that "a hospital is different from other management jobs in that it contains many divisive elements. For the most part, the primary providers of care, the physicians, are not usually employed by the hospital. There are different groups of highly technical employees, a complex physical plant with great energy demands, and a need for fast transfer of information. Furthermore, hospitals are highly regulated. In New York State, more than 160 different regulatory bodies inspect a hospital's affairs."

What Education and Skills Will I Need?

High school: Preparation for college, nursing school, or business college.

College: Most administrators have a business background. Increasingly hospital administrators in urban areas and in large hospitals are required to have a graduate degree for their jobs.

A two-year and four-year degree in health service administration is offered in 60 U.S. colleges and universities. Seventy-five colleges awarded master's degrees in health administration, and 22 awarded master's degrees in public health. A Master of Business Administration (MBA) or a Master of Public Health (MPH) are the top credentials for this career.

Personal skills: According to Norman B. Urmy, Administrator of University Hospital and Vice-president of New York University Medical Center, "Plan to spend 85 percent of your time talking to people, not sitting in your office calling the shots. You'll need an even temper, a liking for people, an ability to tolerate frustration, and a willingness to plan long-term, because great successes demand consensus, and that can take years to achieve."

How Many Health Service Administrators Are There and Where Do They Work?

There are 220,000 health service administrators and almost half are hospital administrators.

$ $ $ $ $

In 1980, administrators in state hospitals with 350 to 800 beds averaged $35,000 a year. Experienced administrators in large health agencies and hospitals earned over $50,000 a year.

What Is the Job Future?

There are about 17,000 hospital administrators, 16,000 administrators of long-term care facilities, 10,000 public health administrators in regulatory agencies such as federal public health services, plus 6,000 others in related areas such as fund-raising agencies for various diseases. About 750 true administrative jobs open up each year. Competition for them is very tough, because there are 85 graduate programs that produce 3,000 qualified applicants a year. Many administrators urge new graduates to start in a large hospital where they will get experience in many systems, or in a Veterans Administration hospital because they have system manuals for everything. In that way, a graduate can learn how an organized operation works before going into private business or to a smaller hospital. Other opportunities for graduates are with the large management-consulting firms, which have divisions specializing in health-care consulting.

RELATED CAREERS

business administrator
social welfare administrator
college administrator

WHERE CAN I GET MORE INFORMATION?

Professional groups

American College of Hospital Administrators
840 North Lake Shore Drive
Chicago, IL 60611

Association of University Programs in Health
One Dupont Circle, NW
Washington, D.C. 20036

Trade journal

Hospitals
American College of Hospital Administrators
840 North Lake Shore Drive
Chicago, IL 60611

MEDICAL RECORDS ADMINISTRATOR

Trains and supervises workers who verify, transcribe, code, and maintain files on patients' medical histories. Develops systems for documenting, storing, and retrieving medical information.

What's It Like to Be a Medical Records Administrator?

Medical records administrators compile statistics and make summaries for reports required by state and health agencies. Medical records include case histories of illnesses, doctors' orders and progress notes, and X-ray and lab reports. Administrators hold meetings with hospital department heads and medical records committees, and plan research projects for the medical team of the hospital.

What Education and Skills Will I Need?

High school: Preparation for college, with emphasis on biological science and computer science.

College: Two or three years of college is usually required before going into one of the 40 approved medical records administration training programs. High school graduates can enter a one-year or two-year college program for medical records technicians. A college degree is required from one of the 44 approved college programs. Programs include anatomy, physiology, hospital administration, and computer science.

Personal skills: Accuracy, interest in detail, ability to write and speak clearly, and ability to be discreet in handling confidential work are needed by medical records administrators.

How Many Medical Records Administrators Are There and Where Do They Work?

There are 15,000 medical records administrators and 6,500 are registered records administrators (RRA). Although most are women, the number of men in the training programs is increasing.

$ $ $ $ $

In 1981, the average starting salary for registered medical records administrators was $18,000 a year. New graduates started with the federal government at $12,300 a year. Experienced administrators averaged about $23,000 a year, with some earning over $30,000 a year.

What Is the Job Future?

There will be very good opportunities for employment through the 1980s. Registered, full-time administrators will get the directors' jobs and best salaries.

RELATED CAREERS

hospital-insurance representative
library director
public health educator

WHERE CAN I GET MORE INFORMATION?

Professional group
American Medical Records Association
875 North Michigan Avenue, Suite 1850
Chicago, IL 60611

Trade journal
Medical Record News
American Medical Records Association
875 North Michigan Avenue, Suite 1850
Chicago, IL 60611

CHIROPRACTOR

Treats patients by manual manipulation of the body, especially the spinal column.

What's It Like to Be a Chiropractor?

Chiropractic is a system for healing based on the principle that a person's health is determined by the nervous system. Chiropractors treat their patients by massage, by using water, light, and heat therapy, and by prescribing diet, exercise, and rest. They do not use drugs or surgery. Howard Riley, chiropractor in a small city, sees about 50 patients a week, from 6 months of age to 90 years of age. He likes the great variety in age and educational background of his patients. He doesn't like the necessary insurance forms, the X-ray forms, and the business operations in general. Dr. Riley advises young people to visit a chiropractor and observe him at work for a day to see what the job is really like.

What Education and Skills Will I Need?

High school: Preparation for college, with as much science as possible.

College: Two years of college are required for admission to the 15 chiropractic colleges approved by the American Chiropractic Association. The degree of Doctor of Chiropractic (D.C.) is awarded after four years of chiropractic college, or six years of training after high school.

Personal skills: Rather than unusual strength, hand dexterity is necessary to be a chiropractor, together with sympathetic understanding.

How Many Chiropractors Are There and Where Do They Work?

There are 23,000 chiropractors. Most of them are in private practice and three-fourths of them practice alone. Half of all chiropractors practice in California, New York, Texas, Missouri, Pennsylvania, and Michigan.

$ $ $ $ $

In 1980, experienced chiropractors averaged $44,000 a year. Beginners made more than $15,000 a year.

What Is the Job Future?

The future work opportunities are expected to be good through the 1980s, even with an increase in new college graduates. The states and regions where chiropractic treatment is still new will be the best places to set up a practice.

RELATED CAREERS

dentist	osteopathic physician
optometrist	podiatrist

WHERE CAN I GET MORE INFORMATION?

Professional group
American Chiropractic Association
American Building
2200 Grand Avenue
Des Moines, IA 50312

Trade journal
Today's Chiropractic
P.O. Box 37
Austell, GA 30001

DENTAL HYGIENIST

Cleans teeth, charts tooth conditions, X-rays teeth, and teaches patients how to maintain good oral health.

What's It Like to Be a Dental Hygienist?

Dental hygienists perform preventive services for patients and teach dental health education. Some hygienists work in public school systems promoting dental health by examining children's teeth and reporting the dental treatment children need to their parents. "I work in a county health department quite independently with my patients in the mornings, and in elementary schools on a dental-health program in the afternoons," writes Gene F. Sanchez, husband and father of two boys, from Michigan. Sanchez also works in the public school system. He likes working with educators in the community, and is frustrated by the poor care most people give their teeth and gums. In his many years at work, including government and private practice, he has found no negative reaction from people to being a male hygienist.

What Education and Skills Will I Need?

High school: Preparation for a two-year dental program, with emphasis on science. Most dental hygienist university programs require the Dental Aptitude Test for admission. The requirements for admission are usually the same as the requirements of the university's four-year programs.

College: Four-year dental hygienist degree programs are available for those who want to go into research or teaching. Each state has its own licensing examination.

Personal skills: Manual dexterity, ability to help people relax under stress, and neatness are necessary in dental hygiene.

How Many Dental Hygienists Are There and Where Do They Work?

There are 36,000 dental hygienists and most of them are women. Three-fourths of the hygienists work in private dentists' offices and one-fourth work for public health or public school systems.

$ $ $ $ $

In 1980, the average salary for a two-year dental hygienist graduate was from $14,000 to $17,000 a year. Beginners earned less.

What Is the Job Future?

The opportunities are expected to be very good through the 1980s. The increase in population and in dental education will create more jobs than the number of hygienists graduating. Many dentists require half-time help or less, providing excellent part-time opportunities for parents with young children or for people with other things to do.

RELATED CAREERS

nurse
nurse anesthetist
medical technologist
radiologic technologist

WHERE CAN I GET MORE INFORMATION?

Professional group
American Dental Association
211 East Chicago Avenue
Chicago, IL 60611

Trade journal
Dental Hygiene
American Dental Association
211 East Chicago Avenue
Chicago, IL 60611

DENTIST

Examines, diagnoses, and treats various oral diseases and abnormalities.

What's It Like to Be a Dentist?

Dentists fill cavities, straighten teeth, take X-rays, and treat gums. They clean and examine teeth and mouths for preventive dentistry. They also extract teeth and substitute artificial dentures designed for the patient. Most of their time is spent with patients; usually their laboratory work is sent out to dental technicians. Dr. Steve Zonies, a young single dentist who has been in practice for three years, finds that being a dentist is a lot harder than he thought it would be. "There is no physical exercise and sitting in one place all day isn't healthy. It pays well, and a dentist can take a lot of time off to do other things. Most people don't like dentists and you have to deal with their fears and worries. Besides that, most patients are smiling when they come in to the office and feel worse when they leave – numb and swollen. The most delight in dentistry is dealing with emergencies, relieving pain, and transforming a totally decayed mouth into a healthy mouth so that a person begins to smile for the first time in years."

What Education and Skills Will I Need?

High school: Preparation for a predental college program, with as much science as possible.

College: Two years of college are required for admission to a four-year dental school. Nearly half now require three years of college and most dental students have a college degree. Predental work includes chemistry, English, biology, and physics.

Personal skills: A good visual memory, excellent judgment of space and shape, a delicate touch, and a high degree of manual dexterity are the necessary skills to be a good dentist.

How Many Dentists Are There and Where Do They Work?

There are 126,000 dentists, and nine out of ten of them are in private practice.

$ $ $ $ $

In 1980, the average income for dentists was about $55,000 a year. In 1981, first-year dentists started with the federal government at $22,500 a year.

What Is the Job Future?

The opportunities for jobs will be good through the 1980s. The more dental care taught in the public schools, the more dental care will be needed. Dentistry is the second-highest paid profession and an excellent career for students with good science marks and an interest in dental care.

RELATED CAREERS

ophthalmologist
doctor
veterinarian

WHERE CAN I GET MORE INFORMATION?

Professional group
American Dental Association
Council on Education
211 East Chicago Avenue
Chicago, IL 60611

Trade journal
ADA News
American Dental Association
211 East Chicago Avenue
Chicago, IL 60611

DOCTOR

Diagnoses diseases and treats people who are ill. Also works in research, in rehabilitation, and in preventive medicine.

What's It Like to Be a Doctor?

Physicians generally examine and treat patients in their own offices and in hospitals. A decreasing percentage of the doctors who provide patient care are general practitioners; the others specialize in one of the 52 fields for which there is graduate training. The largest specialties are internal medicine, general surgery, obstetrics and gynecology, psychiatry, pediatrics, radiology, anesthesiology, ophthalmology, pathology, and orthopedic surgery. Family and community medicine are two more specialties that many medical students are choosing in order to practice family medicine in much the same way as general practitioners used to practice it.

Julius Boenello, single, a surgical resident (paid hospital training after medical school) in a university hospital, says that the residency program is a long, hard, tough program. "The job is never boring, very diverse, with varied activities every day. The work keeps you on your toes." Residents work an average of 100 to 110 hours a week for five years in surgical residency programs. "I spend three to four hours a day in the operating room. The majority of my time is spent on the wards looking after pre- and postoperatives. That's what makes a good surgeon. Anyone can cut, tie, and thread." Boenello stresses that young people will need the ambition to put the necessary time into the training. "You really have to give up your personal life for most of this time. If you're married, you never see your family. If you're single, you don't have a chance to be with friends. But the training is all a means to an end. Brighter days are ahead when you practice on your own."

What Education and Skills Will I Need?

High school: Preparation for college by taking as much science and mathematics as offered. A strong "B" average in the sciences and top motivation for staying in premed and medical school are the main requirements. You don't have to be a genius to go into medicine as many students are led to believe.

College: Premedicine or biology are the usual majors to prepare for one of the 103 medical colleges. In addition to the physical sciences, the behavioral sciences and computer science are becoming more important in medical education. Changes in curriculum include a broader education for clinical work as well as for the classroom. After graduation from a four-year medical school, one year of internship is required to be licensed to practice. Interns are paid by the hospital, and a paid year of residency or specializing in a field of medicine follows the internship.

Personal skills: A strong interest and desire to serve the sick and injured are needed, as are persistence for continued study and ability to make fast decisions in emergencies.

How Many Doctors Are There and Where Do They Work?

There are 405,000 doctors and 87 percent of them are men. Like graduate schools in law and theology, medical schools are very white-male oriented with almost no nonwhite or female faculty.

$ $ $ $ $

Medical school graduates who had completed three years of residency started with the VA hospitals at $38,500 a year in 1981. In addition, they received up to $13,000 in other cash benefits. Experienced male physicians averaged $67,450 a year after taxes, the highest average earning of any occupational group. Female physicians made much less.

What Is the Job Future?

Depending on the locality, opportunities will be good through the 1980s. The shortage of doctors is over. A surplus of 70,000 physicians is predicted. Despite the numbers, it is still difficult to get doctors to work in inner cities and rural areas.

RELATED CAREERS

dentist	audiologist
optometrist	veterinarian

WHERE CAN I GET MORE INFORMATION?

Professional group
Council on Medical Education
American Medical Association
535 North Dearborn Street
Chicago, IL 60610

Trade journal
New England Journal of Medicine
10 Shattuck Street
Boston, MA 02115

NURSE

Observes, assesses, and records symptoms, reactions, and progress of patients; administers medications; helps rehabilitate patients; instructs patients and family members about proper health care; and helps maintain a physical and emotional environment that promotes recovery.

What's It Like to Be a Nurse?

Nurses work with patients and families in a variety of settings. They provide direct care to patients in hospitals and nursing homes by assessing patients' needs and problems, making nursing diagnoses, and planning and implementing nursing actions that enhance patients' recovery. They provide the medical care prescribed by the physician; teach patients about their illness and how to prevent complications; and teach patients how to promote good health practices. Within the hospital setting, there are areas of specialization such as psychiatric nursing, coronary care, intensive care, pediatric nursing, intensive care nursery, and obstetrics.

Nurses who provide direct care of patients are called *staff nurses* or *primary care nurses*. Administrators who provide indirect care to patients are called *head nurses* and/or *coordinators, team leaders,* and *supervisors*. Nurses also provide care to clients and families in the community. *Public health nurses* and *visiting nurses* provide direct care to patients who have been discharged from the hospital; teach health and health practices; provide immunizations; and work with teachers, parents, and doctors in the community, home, and school. *Office nurses* help physicians care for patients in private practices or clinics. *Private duty nurses* work in a patient's home or in the hospital to take care of one patient who needs special and constant attention. After advanced training, *nurse practitioners* provide primary health care as independent decision makers. They often establish a joint practice with a physician or run their own clinics.

A few comments about what it's like for men in nursing: "You seldom see a male nurse on television," says Kenneth Zwolski, a former science teacher who is enrolled in nursing school. "Now that I'm right where the action is, I'm amazed at what's available in terms of future careers. I can do a great variety of jobs as a nurse." Frank Costello, 35 years old and a former social worker, is in a college nursing program. He says, "I think that some men tend to be more sensitive today and they seek a vocation that enhances that quality rather than being in sex-stereotyped roles."

What Education and Skills Will I Need?

High school: Preparation for nursing education, with a college preparatory program and an emphasis in science.

Nursing education: By 1985, members of the nursing profession will be expected to have a minimum of a bachelor's degree in order to practice as a professional nurse. All others will be called technical nurses. There are, however, three types of registered nurse (RN) education: a three-year diploma program conducted by a hospital, a bachelor's degree program in a college, or an associate degree program offered in a two-year junior or community college. Nurses who plan a career in teaching and research will be required to get a doctorate in nursing. There are many opportunities for specialization through a master's program, including a master's in public health for administration careers.

Personal skills: Ability to accept responsibility, initiative, good judgment, good mental and physical stamina, and an ability to make reasoned decisions.

How Many Nurses Are There and Where Do They Work?

There are 1.4 million registered nurses, but only 70 percent are practicing. Three-fourths of the RNs work in hospitals or nursing homes, 40,000 are private duty nurses, 100,000 are

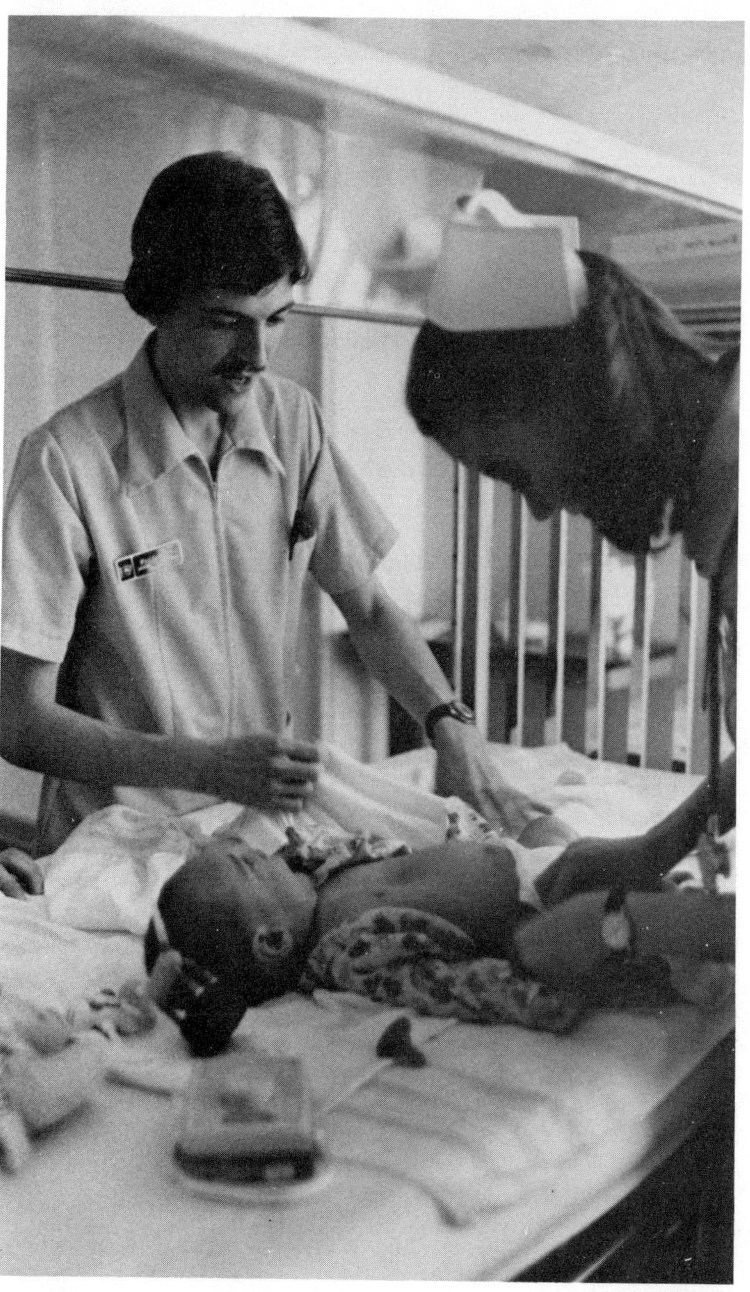

NURSE

office nurses, 120,000 are public health nurses, 20,000 are in industry, and 40,000 are nurse educators.

$ $ $ $ $

In 1980, the average salary for staff and industrial nursing was $17,000 a year. RNs in nursing homes earned less at $14,500 a year. Specialists earned $18,000 to $30,000 a year, educators $20,000 a year, and supervisors to $40,000 a year. The Veterans Administration offered inexperienced nurses with a college degree $15,933 a year as a starting salary.

What Is the Job Future?

Nursing may be one of the most exciting, expansive, developing professions in the next decade. Salaries, advancement, and fringe benefits are increasing rapidly. There will be excellent opportunities through the 1980s for nurses in administration, nursing schools, and clinics. Increasing numbers of men are entering nursing as they learn that the 1.9 percent unemployment rate for nurses is one of the lowest in the entire work force.

RELATED CAREERS

occupational therapist
physical therapist
physician's assistant

WHERE CAN I GET MORE INFORMATION?

Professional groups
American Nurses' Association
2420 Pershing Road
Kansas City, MO 64108

National League for Nursing
10 Columbus Circle
New York, NY 10019

Trade journal
RN Magazine
Litton Publications
Oradell, NJ 07649

OPTOMETRIST

Examines people's eyes for vision problems and disease, and tests eyes for depth, color, and focus perceptions.

What's It Like to Be an Optometrist?

"I work with contact lenses. They change the client's looks completely; when a client is happy with the results, it makes my day," says optometrist Geno Frattini, father of three preschool children. "I work from 8 a.m. in the morning until 6 p.m. at night, and I like every aspect of my work. I'm my own boss and I make all the decisions. The most exciting part of the work is when I hold up different lenses for children and ask them what they can see, and they give me a 'cat ate the canary' grin, suddenly realizing the things they haven't seen clearly before."

What Education and Skills Will I Need?

High school: Preparation for college, with an emphasis on science.

College: Two years of college are required for admission to the four-year program of the College of Optometry to become a Doctor of Optometry (O.D.). Subjects required in college are English, mathematics, biology, physics, and chemistry. There are 13 approved schools of optometry in the United States.

Personal skills: Business ability (most optometrists are self-employed), self-discipline, and tact with patients are needed.

How Many Optometrists Are There and Where Do They Work?

There are 27,000 optometrists and 97 percent of them are men. Most optometrists are self-employed and half of them work in the following five states: California, Illinois, New York, Pennsylvania, and Ohio. To offset high costs of establishing a practice, there is a growing trend toward partnerships and group practice.

$ $ $ $ $

In 1980, the starting income for beginners was $18,000 a year. Experienced optometrists averaged $45,000 annually.

What Is the Job Future?

Employment opportunities will be favorable through the 1980s. Very few careers pay as well, award a doctorate only six years after high school, and have as good part-time opportunities as does optometry.

RELATED CAREERS

chiropractor	podiatrist
dentist	veterinarian

WHERE CAN I GET MORE INFORMATION?

Professional group
American Optometric Association
243 Lindbergh Boulevard
St. Louis, MO 63141

Trade journal
Optometric Management
20 Harlan Avenue
White Plains, NY 10603

OSTEOPATHIC PHYSICIAN

Diagnoses and treats diseases with special emphasis on the musculoskeletal system—bones, muscles, ligaments, and nerves.

What's It Like to Be an Osteopathic Physician?

One of the basic treatments used by osteopathic physicians centers on manipulating the musculoskeletal system with the hands. Osteopathic physicians also use surgery, drugs, and all other accepted methods of medical care. Most osteopathic physicians are in family practice and engage in general medicine. These physicians usually see patients in their offices, make house calls, and treat patients in one of the 200 osteopathic hospitals.

What Education and Skills Will I Need?

High school: Preparation for college, with science and mathematics courses.

College: Most osteopathic students have a college degree, with courses that include biology, chemistry, physics, and English, to qualify for a three-year or four-year program in one of the 14 schools of osteopathy.

Personal skills: A strong interest in osteopathic principles of healing, a keen sense of touch, and self-confidence are needed.

How Many Osteopathic Physicians Are There and Where Do They Work?

There are 18,750 osteopathic physicians and 87 percent of them are men. Almost 85 percent are in private practice chiefly in states with osteopathic hospitals. Three-fifths of all osteopathic physicians practice in Florida, Michigan, Pennsylvania, New Jersey, Ohio, Texas, and Missouri.

$ $ $ $ $

In 1981, graduates of a residency program started at $38,000 a year with VA hospitals. In addition, they received up to $13,000 in other cash benefits.

What Is the Job Future?

Chances for work will be very good through the 1980s, especially in states with osteopathic hospitals.

RELATED CAREERS

chiropractor	optometrist
dentist	veterinarian

WHERE CAN I GET MORE INFORMATION?

Professional group
American Association of Colleges of Osteopathic Medicine
4720 Montgomery Lane
Bethesda, MD 20814

Trade journal
The Osteopathic Physician
122 East 42 Street
New York, NY 10017

PODIATRIST

Prevents, diagnoses, and treats foot diseases and injuries.

What's It Like to Be a Podiatrist?

Podiatrists take X-rays and perform pathological tests to help in diagnoses. They perform foot surgery, fit corrective devices, and prescribe drugs, physical therapy, and proper shoes. They treat corns, bunions, calluses, ingrown toe nails, skin and nail diseases, deformed toes, and arch disabilities. Most podiatrists are generalists and provide all types of foot care.

What Education and Skills Will I Need?

High school: Preparation for college, with strong science and mathematics.

College: Most podiatric medicine students are college graduates and go on to one of the five podiatric schools for four years.

Personal skills: Manual dexterity, scientific interest, ability for detailed work, and a pleasant personality are all helpful for success in podiatry.

How Many Podiatrists Are There and Where Do They Work?

There are 12,000 podiatrists and most are in private practice in large cities.

$ $ $ $ $

In 1980, the VA hospitals offered $22,486 a year to new graduates. Established podiatrists earned over $50,000 a year.

What Is the Job Future?

Chances for work are very good. The increase in sports medicine and numbers of joggers, the older populations, and a trend toward providing preventive foot care for children will increase the number of jobs.

RELATED CAREERS

- chiropractor
- doctor
- osteopathic physician
- dentist
- veterinarian

WHERE CAN I GET MORE INFORMATION?

Professional group
American Association of Colleges of Podiatric Medicine
20 Chevy Chase Circle, NW
Washington, D.C. 20015

Trade journal
Journal of Podiatry Association
American Association of Colleges of Podiatric Medicine
20 Chevy Chase Circle, NW
Washington, D.C. 20015

VETERINARIAN

Prevents, diagnoses, treats, and controls diseases and injuries of animals.

What's It Like to Be a Veterinarian?

Veterinarians treat animals in hospitals and clinics or on the farm or ranch. They perform surgery on sick and injured animals and prescribe and administer drugs, medicines, and vaccines. A large number of vets specialize in the health and breeding of cattle, poultry, sheep, swine, or horses. Their work is important for the nation's food production and also for public health. Seth Whitcome, 74-year-old veterinarian in Iowa, says that young people should keep in mind that once a vet starts in private practice, he can keep working as long as he feels like doing so. "Most of my friends are long since retired, but I can cut down my practice, and put in the time to bring in the money I need to make ends meet."

What Education and Skills Will I Need?

High school: Preparation for college, with emphasis on biological sciences.

College: Two or three years of preveterinary medicine is required for admission into a four-year college of veterinary medicine.

Personal skills: Ability to communicate with animals and love of the outdoors are important for a vet, as is interest in food, health, and science.

How Many Veterinarians Are There and Where Do They Work?

There are 35,000 vets and 7 out of 10 are in private practice. The type of practice generally varies according to geography. Veterinarians in rural areas mainly treat farm animals; those in small towns are usually in general practice; those in cities and suburban areas often limit their practice to pets.

$ $ $ $ $

In 1981, the federal government started veterinarians at $21,065 a year. The average income for veterinarians with the federal government was $34,100 a year. Private practice pays more, and self-employed vets start with less money but usually make much more than veterinarians on a salary.

RELATED CAREERS

chiropractor	doctor
dentist	podiatrist
optometrist	

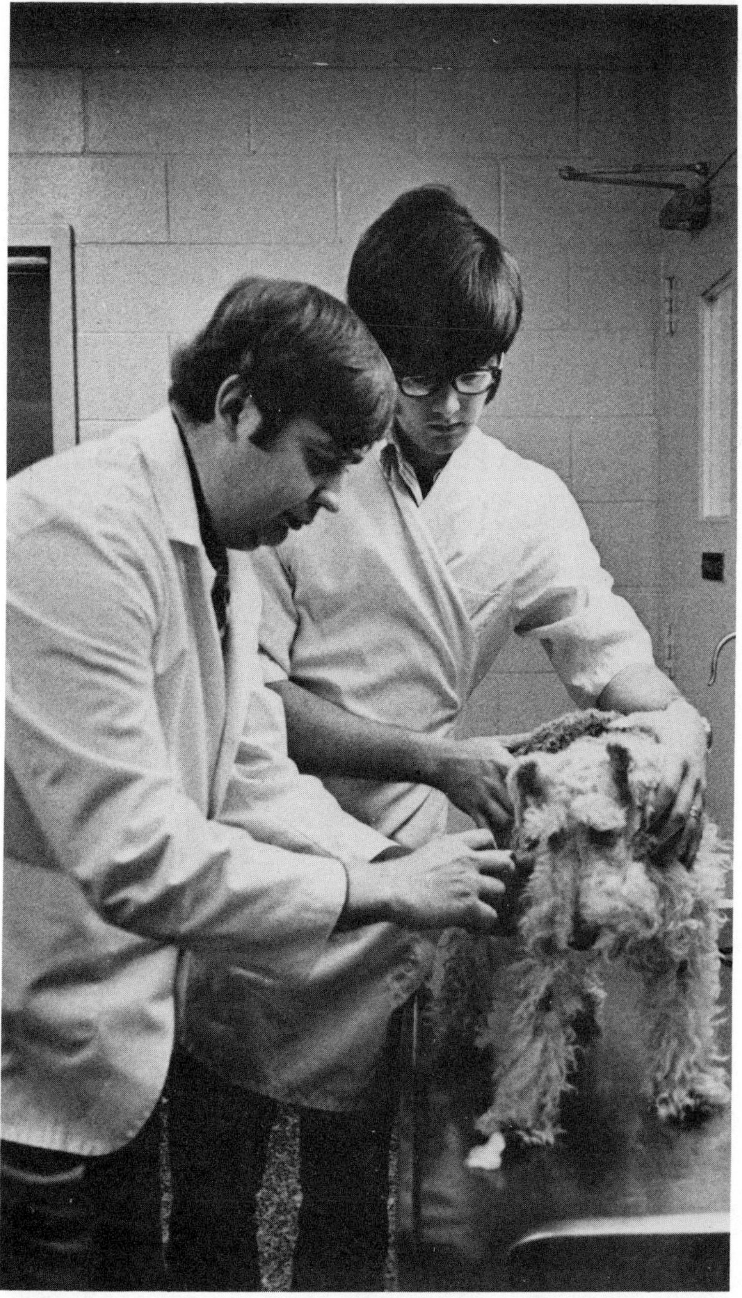

VETERINARIAN

WHERE CAN I GET MORE INFORMATION?

Professional group
American Veterinary Medical Association
930 North Meacham Road
Schaumburg, IL 60172

Trade journal
Veterinary Economics
2728 Euclid Avenue
Cleveland, Ohio 44115

OCCUPATIONAL THERAPIST

Helps patients adjust to their disabilities; plans and directs activities to help patients return to work.

What's It Like to Be an Occupational Therapist?

An occupational therapist works as a member of a medical team with a doctor, physical therapist, vocational counselor, nurse, and social worker. He teaches manual and creative skills such as weaving, clay modeling, leather working, commercial skills, and power tools. The goals of the therapist are to help patients to gain stability, combat boredom during long illnesses, and develop independence in routine daily skills such as eating, dressing, and writing. "The biggest problem of being a man in a woman's world," says Julio Gagetti, "is that the money isn't there. For the time being, I'll stay in occupational therapy until I can't afford the luxury of a job I like so much."

What Education and Skills Will I Need?

High school: Preparation for college, with emphasis on science, crafts, and social science.

College: Fifty-three colleges and universities offer a degree in occupational therapy. Many college graduates go into occupational therapy after college from a variety of majors—often biology or physical education—and get a master's degree in occupational therapy in one year.

Personal skills: An advocate's attitude toward the sick and disabled, manual skills, maturity, patience, and imagination are needed.

How Many Occupational Therapists Are There and Where Do They Work?

There are 19,000 occupational therapists and only 10 percent are men. Over half of all therapists work in hospitals; the remainder work in rehabilitation centers, homes for the aged, nursing homes, schools, and special workshops for the disabled.

$ $ $ $ $

In 1981, the average salaries were from $19,000 to $23,000 a year. Directors earned more than $30,000 a year, and beginners with the federal government started at $13,700 a year.

What Is the Job Future?

The future is expected to be very good through the 1980s. The increase in community health centers, long-term health care facilities, and home health care will add to the number of jobs. Part-time opportunities are also very good.

RELATED CAREERS

physical therapist
prosthetist
speech pathologist

WHERE CAN I GET MORE INFORMATION?

Professional group
American Occupational Therapy Association
1383 Piccard Drive
Rockville, MD 20850

PHYSICAL THERAPIST

Uses exercise, massage, heat, water, and electricity to treat and rehabilitate people with disabilities.

What's It Like to Be a Physical Therapist?

Physical therapists perform and interpret tests and measurements for muscle strength, motor development, functional capacity, and respiratory and circulatory efficiency. They plan a program of therapy to include exercises for increasing strength, endurance, and coordination; stimuli to make motor activity and learning easier; instructions to carry out everyday activity; and applications of massage, heat and cold, light, water, or electricity to relieve pain or improve the condition of muscles. Ernie Nalette, father of a new baby, says what he likes best about being a physical therapist is the great variety of patients he deals with—accident victims, crippled children, disabled older persons, cardiac rehabilitation patients, chest patients, and more. He also likes the interaction with other health care people working together on his patients.

What Education and Skills Will I Need?

High school: Preparation for college, with emphasis on science.

College: Most students major in physical therapy in college and graduate with a degree in physical therapy. A one-year course is offered for college graduates, usually in connection with a hospital program. Many physical education majors and science majors go into this program. There are 57 approved schools of physical therapy in the United States.

Personal skills: Resourcefulness, patience, manual dexterity, physical stamina, and an ability to work with disabled people and their families are needed to be good in physical therapy.

How Many Physical Therapists Are There and Where Do They Work?

One-fourth of the 34,000 licensed physical therapists are men. About half of the therapists work in general hospitals; others work in nursing homes, rehabilitation centers, home health agencies, clinics, and the armed forces.

PHYSICAL THERAPIST

$ $ $ $ $

In 1981, beginning physical therapists averaged $17,000 a year. Experienced therapists averaged from $21,600 to $27,000 a year.

What Is the Job Future?

The opportunities will remain excellent through the 1980s. New graduates are in great demand, as there are not enough therapists for the growing number of jobs.

RELATED CAREERS

occupational therapist
speech therapist
prosthetist
respiratory therapist

WHERE CAN I GET MORE INFORMATION?

Professional group
American Physical Therapy Association
1156 15th Street, NW
Washington, D.C. 20005

Trade journal
Physical Therapist
American Physical Therapy Association
1156 15th Street, NW
Washington, D.C. 20005

SPEECH AND HEARING THERAPIST

Diagnoses and treats people with the inability to speak or hear clearly.

What's It Like to Be a Speech and Hearing Therapist?

A speech and hearing therapist, sometimes called a speech pathologist and audiologist, works with children or adults who have communication disorders (speech, hearing, language, learning). This work may be with one person or with small groups. Lessons vary from one-half hour to group classes of two hours, and handle problems of stuttering, defective articulation, brain damage, mental retardation, or emotional disturbance. The responsibility of the therapist is to identify and evaluate the disorder; consult with the other specialists involved, such as the physician, psychologist, social worker, or counselor; and organize a program of therapy.

What Education and Skills Will I Need?

High school: Preparation for college, with a strong science program.

College: Major in speech pathology and audiology, or in any related field such as education, psychology, or education for the blind or deaf, to prepare for graduate school. A master's degree from one of the 230 college programs is required for professional certification in most states. Many scholarships and fellowships are available for graduate school through the United States Vocational Rehabilitation Administration.

Personal skills: Patience with slow progress, responsibility, objectivity, ability to work with detail, and concern for the needs of others are important for therapists.

How Many Speech and Hearing Therapists Are There and Where Do They Work?

One-fourth of the 35,000 speech and hearing therapists are men. About half work for the public school systems and clinical service centers. The rest work in hospitals, clinics, agencies, and private practice.

$ $ $ $ $

In 1981, the average salary in hospitals and medical centers was $17,000 a year. The federal government started therapists with a master's degree at $18,600 a year. Experienced therapists averaged $21,300 a year.

What Is the Job Future?

Job opportunities will be good through the 1980s. Increased emphasis on learning disabilities in elementary education will create jobs. Best chances for work will be for M.A. graduates outside of metropolitan areas.

RELATED CAREERS

occupational therapist
optometrist
physical therapist

WHERE CAN I GET MORE INFORMATION?

Professional group
American Speech and Hearing Association
10801 Rockville Pike
Bethesda, MD 20852

Trade journal
Audiology and Hearing Education
15300 Ventura Boulevard, Suite 301
Sherman Oaks, CA 91403

DIETITIAN

Plans nutritious meals to help people maintain or recover good health.

What's It Like to Be a Dietitian?

The hospital dietitian supervises tray service to patients, selects foods, and plans general menus that meet nutritional requirements for health or medical treatment. The dietitian plans modified meals for the following day, teaches special diets to hospital patients and outpatients, and consults with doctors and nurses concerning the special needs of patients who must also take prescribed drugs. The primary responsibility of the dietitian is to teach other professionals in the hospital the value of nutrition for patients trying to recover good health. Because a hospital functions 24 hours a day, 365 days a year, a dietitian's schedule includes all hours and all days.

What Education and Skills Will I Need?

High school: Preparation for college, with an emphasis on science and computer science.

College: Preparation for a degree in foods and nutrition or in institutional management. To qualify for professional recognition, take one of the 68 approved one-year internships in a hospital. Most of the top jobs are offered to students who have completed the internship, which provides further education and on-the-job experience under supervision.

Personal skills: An aptitude for science and organizational and administrative abilities are needed.

How Many Dietitians Are There and Where Do They Work?

There are 44,000 full-time dietitians and 10 percent of them are men. About half of all dietitians work in hospitals, including Veterans Administration and U.S. Public Health Service. Colleges, universities, and public schools employ almost half of the dietitians, while a few work in large business cafeterias and the Armed Forces. Part-time opportunities are very good, with 15 percent of all dietitians working part-time.

$ $ $ $ $

In 1981, beginning salaries of new graduates of an internship program averaged $15,800 a year. Experienced dietitians in hospitals earned as much as $25,872 a year.

What Is the Job Future?

Full-time and part-time job opportunities will be very good through the 1980s. The increase in all health institutions and nursing homes and the increase in population will mean more jobs available than the number of graduates in dietetics. Small hospitals and small institutions often hire part-time dietitians.

RELATED CAREERS

food technologist
home economist
food service manager

WHERE CAN I GET MORE INFORMATION?

Professional group
The American Dietetic Association
430 North Michigan Avenue
Chicago, IL 60611

Trade journal
Journal of Nutrition
9650 Rockville Pike
Bethesda, MD 20014

MEDICAL TECHNOLOGIST

Performs chemical, microscopic, and bacteriological tests under the supervision of a pathologist to diagnose the causes and nature of disease.

What's It Like to Be a Medical Technologist?

Medical technologists perform blood count, blood-cholesterol level, and skin tests. They also examine other body fluids and tissues microscopically for bacteria, fungus, and other organisms. In small hospitals, the medical technologists do all of the tests; in larger hospitals, they specialize in an area such as the study of blood cells or tissue preparation and examination. Medical technologists are usually assisted by medical technicians and laboratory assistants who perform simple, routine tests. Because of the computer revolution, the tasks of medical technologists are rapidly changing as routine tests are performed by computer. Now more specialization is required of the technologist.

What Education and Skills Will I Need?

High school: Preparation for college, with emphasis in science and mathematics.

College: A college degree program or one year of special training after three years of college is required. Chemistry, biology, mathematics, and computer science are required courses.

Personal skills: Manual dexterity and good eyesight are essential, as well as accuracy, dependability, and the ability to work under pressure.

How Many Medical Technologists Are There and Where Do They Work?

There are 50,000 medical technologists and only about 8,000 are men; however, the number of men has been increasing in the last few years. The majority work in hospitals and some work in health agencies and research.

$ $ $ $ $

In 1980, the average starting salary was $13,200 a year. Experienced technologists averaged $16,000 a year.

What Is the Job Future?

General medical technology is not in demand because computer systems can do the routine tests cheaper and more efficiently. The demands now are for those with advanced technological skills. The opportunities for specialists will be very good through the 1980s. Technologists with a degree and specialty will have the best chances for supervising other lab workers.

RELATED CAREERS

chemistry technologist
criminologist
food tester

WHERE CAN I GET MORE INFORMATION?

Professional groups

American Medical Technologists
710 Higgins Road
Park Ridge, IL 60068

American Society of Medical Technology
330 Meadowfern Drive
Houston, TX 77067

Registry of Medical Technologists
American Society of Clinical Pathologists
P.O. Box 11270
Chicago, IL 60612

Trade journal
Journal of Medical Technologists
710 Higgins Road
Park Ridge, IL 60068

PHARMACIST

Selects, compounds, dispenses, and preserves drugs and medicines to fill the prescriptions of physicians and dentists.

What's It Like to Be a Pharmacist?

Hospital pharmacist Bob Coughlin, recently out of school and living with a friend, works all three shifts at the pharmacy at different times during the week. "Most of my work," he says, "is mechanical—filling prescriptions, checking technicians' work, and answering questions for doctors and nurses on the telephone about drugs. However, as we work, we also check all drug orders for drug interaction and misdosage. This aspect of my job is done with the hospital's computer terminal." Coughlin reads professional journals and attends seminars to try to keep up to date on new drugs marketed every day. He finds it discouraging not to meet the patient he fills a perscription for, especially since he is often asked to suggest a change in or to monitor the patient's therapy. "It's rewarding to have your suggestions used, but one can't expect a great sense of daily accomplishment or thanks from doctors and nurses, who often see the pharmacist only as someone to fill prescriptions rather than as part of the health team." Coughlin likes best to use his knowledge of drugs to monitor a patient's therapy. In the future, he hopes to become more actively involved in "the health care team."

What Education and Skills Will I Need?

High School: Preparation for college, with biology, chemistry, and computer science courses.

College: Pharmacy is a five-year college program leading to a degree. The program includes chemistry, physics, mathematics, computer science, zoology, and physiology. Each state requires its own license to practice.

Personal skills: Business ability, an interest in medicine, orderliness, accuracy, and the ability to build the confidence of customers are needed for success in pharmacy.

How Many Pharmacists Are There and Where Do They Work?

There are 141,000 licensed pharmacists, 96,000 work in local drugstores and 25,000 own their own stores. Others work for hospitals, pharmaceutical manufacturers, and wholesalers.

$ $ $ $ $

Pharmacy pays better than most health-related careers that require the same level of education. In 1981, beginning pharmacists earned $15,200 a year with the federal government. In hospitals, they earned $21,000 a year, and much more in retail business. Experienced pharmacists in hospitals and medical centers averaged $27,200 a year.

What Is the Job Future?

The best opportunities will be in hospitals and health facilities. Many localities will have many more pharmacists than jobs. The drug business, medical research, and government subsidies of medical bills will continue to rapidly increase the demand for pharmacists.

RELATED CAREERS

pharmaceutical chemist
pharmaceutical sales representative
pharmacologist

PHARMACIST

WHERE CAN I GET MORE INFORMATION?

Professional groups

American Pharmaceutical Association
2215 Constitution Avenue, NW
Washington, D.C. 20037

American Council on Pharmaceutical Education
One East Wacker Drive
Chicago, IL 60601

Trade journal

American Druggist
Stanley Sieglman
224 West 57 Street
New York, NY 10019

SCIENCE AND TECHNOLOGY

Astronomer
Biologist
Chemist
Conservationist
Engineer
Environmental Scientist
Food Scientist
Mathematician
Physicist

About these careers *More than 3 million people, or nearly one-quarter of all professional workers, are engineers, scientists, or other scientific and technical workers. The number of scientists and engineers has tripled in the past twenty-five years. Careers for more than two million jobs are described in this cluster.*

A bachelor's degree is usually needed to enter scientific and engineering jobs. In mathematics and the physical and biological sciences, more emphasis is placed on advanced degrees. For some careers, such as astronomer, a doctorate is required for full professional status. Undergraduate training for scientists and engineers includes courses in their major field and in related science areas, including mathematics. Courses and skills in computer science are important for all engineers and scientists, and students are also required to take courses in English and a foreign language.

Students who want to specialize in a particular area of science should select their schools carefully. For example, those who plan to become biomedical engineers or biochemists and work in medicine should study at a university affiliated with a hospital. Those who want to be agricultural scientists can get the most practical training at state universities with agricultural experiment stations.

Working conditions in scientific and technical careers, such as forester, range manager, engineer, geologist, and meteorologist, can involve considerable time away from home working outdoors in remote parts of the country. Foresters may also work extra hours on emergency duty, such as in firefighting or on search-and-rescue missions. Many engineers spend some time in a factory or mine, at a construction site, or at some other outdoor location. Others work under quiet conditions in modern offices and research laboratories. Exploration geologists often work overseas. They travel to remote sites by helicopter and jeep, and cover large areas by foot, often working in teams. Geologists in mining sometimes work underground. Meteorologists in small weather stations generally work alone; those in large stations work as part of a team.

New engineering graduates begin working under the close supervision of experienced engineers. To determine the specialities for which graduates are best suited, many companies have special programs to acquaint new engineers with industrial practices. Experienced engineers may advance to positions of greater responsibility; those with proven ability often become administrators, and in increasingly larger numbers are being promoted to top management jobs. Some engineers obtain Masters of Business Administration (MBAs) to improve their advancement opportunities, while others obtain law degrees and become patent attorneys.

Science and technology are fields with the most jobs. These jobs are the careers of the computer age. If you want to get the best job opportunities, think seriously about science and technology. Whatever your career choice, add some technical skills to your credentials so that you can translate the arts, business, or social sciences into a computer-age career.

ASTRONOMER

Uses the principles of physics and mathematics to study and determine the behavior of matter and energy in outer space.

What's It Like to Be an Astronomer?

Astronomers collect and analyze data of the sun, moon, planets, and stars to determine the size, shape, temperature, composition, and motion of these bodies. They compute the positions of the planets and make statistical studies of the stars. In addition to gathering information by telescope, they increasingly gather information by rockets and earth satellites that carry cameras and measuring devices. Bradford A. Smith, leader of Voyager I's imaging team, finds Saturn "the most bedeviling thing in the sky. The mystery of the rings keeps getting deeper and deeper, until we think it's a bottomless pit. The thing I least expected to see was an eccentric ring—and we have found two." Astronomers have to "think on their feet" as the data come in. They work on teams, consulting with academics such as Professor Peter Goldreich, California Institute of Technology, known as one of the very best scientists to probe the dynamics of the solar system. They also work with numbers collected by Voyager I in its Saturn exploration. Mission Chief Scientist Edward C. Stone, who was in charge of collecting Saturnian wind speeds and directions, has said, "Until you have numbers, you don't have a science."

What Education and Skills Will I Need?

High school: Preparation for a physical science major in college by taking as much mathematics, physical science, and computer science as high school offers.

College: Many astronomers major in mathematics or physics as undergraduates. A master's degree in astronomy is necessary for beginning jobs, but you must have a Ph.D. for the top positions and a career in astronomy.

Personal skills: Perseverance, the ability to concentrate on detail, and the ability to work alone are needed in astronomy.

How Many Astronomers Are There and Where Do They Work?

Astronomy is the smallest physical science, with only 3,000 professional astronomers. Over half of this number teach and do research in colleges and universities.

$ $ $ $ $

In 1980, the average salary for astronomers was $26,000 a year. Industry will pay more as its demand for astronomers increases. The average salary for space scientists with the federal government was $38,000 a year.

What Is the Job Future?

There are many more astronomers than jobs and federal money for research has been drastically cut. Expect keen competition through the 1980s for this work. Those who have had some summer or part-time experience will have the best chances for jobs.

RELATED CAREERS

physicist
other physical scientists
mathematician

WHERE CAN I GET MORE INFORMATION?

Professional group
The American Astronomical Society
University of Delaware
Newark, DE 19711

Trade journals
Sky and Telescope
Sky Publications Corp.
49 Bay State Road
Cambridge, MA 02138

Weatherwise
American Meteorological Society
45 Beacon Street
Boston, MA 02108

BIOLOGIST

Studies the structure, evolution, behavior, and life processes of living organisms.

What's it Like to Be a Biologist?

Major industry is just beginning to find applications for the new biology, that is, genetic engineering to manufacture living materials. For example, bacteria are being used to convert sunlight into electrochemical energy, and new life forms of bacteria are being bred to replace nuclear power plants. More traditional biologists are working to improve medicine, to increase crop yields, and to improve our natural environment. The biological sciences include many specialities, such as botanists who study all aspects of plant life, and zoologists who study animal life and usually specialize in birds, insects, or mammals. The bigger fields of biological specialization are genetics, horticulture, nutrition, and pharmacology. Biological scientists usually work in the field or in a laboratory with a team of scientists, publish their findings, and also teach. Sometimes called life scientists, they study all aspects of living organisms, emphasizing the relationship of animals and plants to their environment. Creating entirely new foods and fibers by cheap and simple methods will be the biologists' work of the 1980s.

What Education and Skills Will I Need?

High school: Preparation for college and graduate school, with as much science, mathematics, and computer science as offered in high school.

College: Major in any biological science and get as broad an understanding as possible of all sciences, including chemistry, physics, and computer science. Choose your graduate school by the particular biological program it offers. A Ph.D is required for research jobs, university teaching, and a career in biological science.

Personal skills: Independent working skills, ability to work with a team, and good communication skills are necessary for the biologist.

How Many Biologists Are There and Where Do They Work?

The biological sciences, including agricultural (35,000) sciences, number 125,000 people, plus 16,000 biochemists. Half of the biologists are employed in colleges, with many in medical schools and state agricultural colleges. One-fourth work in private industry, such as drug and food companies, and another fourth work with the federal government in the Department of Agriculture.

$ $ $ $ $

In 1981, private industry offered an average of $15,200 a year for biologists with bachelors' degrees. Biologists with masters' degrees began at $15,193 or $18,585 a year with the federal government. Average salaries for all biologists with the federal government were $28,100 a year.

What Is the Job Future?

From Toffler's *The Third Wave* comes the observation that biology will replace chemistry in the next thirty years. Biologists will be involved with solutions to the energy problem; converting the ocean into food for the world; eliminating the need for oil in plastics, paint, and other manufactured products; and genetic engineering. Biologists will be on the cutting edge of the technical revolution, where future opportunities are just beginning to explode in many directions.

RELATED CAREERS

forester
soil conservationist
oceanographer

WHERE CAN I GET MORE INFORMATION?

Professional groups
American Institute of Biological Sciences
1401 Wilson Boulevard
Arlington, VA 22209

American Society of Biological Chemists
9650 Rockville Pike
Bethesda, MD 20014

American Society of Horticultural Science
701 North Saint Asaph Street
Alexandria, VA 22314

Trade journal
American Naturalist
University of Chicago Press
5801 Ellis Avenue
Chicago, IL 60637

CHEMIST

Studies the properties and composition of matter; often performs chemical tests on manufactured goods such as drugs, plastics, dyes, paint, and petroleum products.

What's It Like to Be a Chemist?

In basic research, a chemist investigates ways to create or improve new products. The process of developing a product begins with descriptions of needed items. If similar products exist, the chemist tests samples to determine their ingredients. If no such product exists, experimentation with various substances yields a product with the required specifications. Chemists usually specialize to become one of the following: An *analytical chemist,* who determines the composition and nature of substances; an *organic chemist,* who studies the chemistry of living things; an *inorganic chemist,* who studies compounds other than carbon; a *physical chemist,* who studies energy; and a *biochemist,* who studies life science. Ph.D. Ron Kepler, a 27-year-old chemist, loves his work but finds his single lifestyle very lonely. He has been transferred to four different labs in four different locations in the past three years. He is never anywhere long enough to get to know people outside of work. He is seriously considering not taking the next promotion, if it means moving again.

What Education and Skills Will I Need?

High school: Preparation for college, with as much science, mathematics, and computer science as you can get in your high school.

College: Over 1,100 colleges offer a bachelor's degree in chemistry. Mathematics and physics are required of all chemists. A Ph.D. and computer skills are necessary for the top jobs in research and university teaching.

Personal skills: Math and science skills, ability to build scientific apparatus by hand, and ability to concentrate on details are essential to the chemist.

How Many Chemists Are There and Where Do They Work?

There are 113,000 chemists and 80 percent of them are men. Sixty-six percent of all chemists work in private industry, and half of these work for chemical manufacturing industries. Many chemists are employed by the food, petroleum, paper, and electrical equipment companies. Twenty percent of all chemists teach in colleges. The industrial states of New York, New Jersey, California, Pennsylvania, Ohio, and Illinois employ half of all chemists.

$ $ $ $ $

In 1981, private industry started college graduates at $19,600 a year, master's degree graduates at $23,600 a year, and Ph.D.s at $29,800 a year. Experienced chemists with Ph.D.s averaged $35,000 a year.

What Is the Job Future?

College teaching jobs will be few, but chances for jobs in private industry to develop new products will be good for chemists at all levels through the 1980s. The increased number of chemists is resulting in competition for jobs with the big companies.

RELATED CAREERS

biochemist
genetic engineer
food scientist

WHERE CAN I GET MORE INFORMATION?

Professional group
American Chemical Society
1155 16th Street, NW
Washington, D.C. 20036

Trade journal
Chemical Technology
American Chemical Society
1155 16th Street, NW
Washington, D.C. 20036

CONSERVATIONIST

Manages, develops, and protects forest, rangelands, wildlife, soil, and water resources.

What's It Like to Be a Conservationist?

Foresters often specialize in timber management, outdoor recreation, or forest economics. They deal with one of our most important natural resources, wood, which is becoming more valuable as it is increasingly used for heat and energy. Range managers, sometimes called range conservationists, range scientists, or range ecologists, determine the number and kind of animals to be grazed, the grazing system to be used, and the best season for grazing, in order to yield a high production in livestock. At the same time, they must conserve soil and vegetation for other uses, such as wildlife grazing, outdoor recreation, and timber production. Soil conservationists help farmers and ranchers with conservation of soil and water. They prepare maps with the soil, water, and vegetation plans of the farmer's land, recommend ways land can best be used, and help estimate costs and returns on land use. Chip Williams, graduate student in forestry economics, has really enjoyed his college studies since committing himself to a specific career. He says, "Now all of my course work has a purpose and falls into place. What excites me about forestry is the scientific knowledge. I thought it was a little more 'back-woodsy' than it is. I spend most of my waking hours thinking about things relating to forestry."

What Education and Skills Will I Need?

High school: Preparation for college, with as much science as possible.

CONSERVATIONIST

College: Major in one of the 43 approved forestry programs, or one of the 20 universities with a range science major. An advanced degree is necessary for teaching and research jobs in conservation.

Personal skills: A love for the outdoors, physical hardiness, and a scientific curiosity to solve problems is needed to be happy in conservation.

How Many Conservationists Are There and Where Do They Work?

There are 30,000 professional foresters, 4,000 range managers, and 5,000 soil conservationists in the country. One-fourth of the foresters are employed by the federal government in the Department of Agriculture, and one-third are in private industry, mainly in the pulp, paper, and lumber companies. Most range managers and soil conservationists work for the government.

$ $ $ $ $

In private industry, beginning foresters averaged $15,200 a year in 1980, and the overall average salary was $25,200 a year. In 1981, a master's degree graduate started with the federal government at $15,193 a year. The average salary for experienced conservationists in state government was $20,400 a year.

What Is the Job Future?

The jobs are increasing in conservation, but the number of foresters and range managers is increasing faster. A competitive job market is expected through the 1980s. Major cuts in federal spending limit the growth of these jobs.

RELATED CAREERS

oceanographer
biologist
environmental scientist
food scientist

WHERE CAN I GET MORE INFORMATION?

Professional groups

American Forestry Association
1319 18th Street, NW
Washington, D.C. 20036

Society for Range Management
2760 West Fifth Avenue
Denver, CO 80204

Soil Conservation Service
U.S. Department of Agriculture
P.O. Box 2890
Washington, D.C. 20013

Trade journals
National Wildlife
1412 16th Street, NW
Washington, D.C. 20036

Forest Industries
500 Howard Street
San Francisco, CA 94105

ENGINEER

Converts raw materials and power into useful products at a reasonable cost in time and money.

What's It Like to Be an Engineer?

Engineers develop electric-power, water-supply, and waste-disposal systems to meet the problems of urban living. They design machines, artificial organs, and industrial machinery and equipment used to manufacture heating, air-conditioning, and ventilation equipment. Engineers also develop scientific equipment to probe outer space and the ocean depths, and they design, plan, and supervise the construction of buildings, highways, and transit systems. They design and develop consumer products such as cars, television sets, video games, and systems for control and automation of business and manufacturing processes.

Most engineers specialize in one of the more than 25 specialties. Within the major specialites are over 85 subdivisions. For example, structural, environmental, hydraulic, and highway engineering are subdivisions of civil engineering. Engineers within each of the branches may apply their specialized knowledge to many fields. For instance, electrical engineers work in medicine, computers, missile guidance, and electric power distribution. Since knowledge of basic engineering principles is

ENGINEER

required for all areas of engineering, it is possible for engineers to shift from one branch or field of specialization to another, especially during the early stages of their careers.

There are six large engineering specialties. *Aerospace engineers* (68,000) work on all types of aircraft and spacecraft, including missiles, rockets, and military and commercial planes. They develop aerospace products, from initial planning and design to final assembly and testing. *Chemical engineers* (55,000) design equipment and chemical plants, and determine methods of manufacturing products. Often, they design and operate pilot plans to test their work, and develop chemical processes such as those for removing chemical contaminants from waste materials. *Civil engineers* (165,000) design and supervise the construction of roads, harbors, airports, tunnels, bridges, water-supply systems, sewage systems, and buildings. *Electrical engineers* (325,000) design, develop, and supervise the manufacturing of electrical and electronic equipment, including electric motors and generators, communications equipment, heart pacemakers, pollution-measuring instrumentation, radar, computers, lasers, missile-guidance systems, and electrical appliances of all kinds. *Industrial engineers* (115,000) design systems for data processing and apply operations-research techniques to organizational, production, and related problems. They also develop management control systems to aid in financial planning and cost analysis; they design production planning and control systems, and design or improve systems to distribute goods and services. *Mechanical engineers* (213,000) design and develop machines that produce power, such as internal combustion engines and nuclear reactors. They also design and develop a great variety of machines that use power, such as refrigeration and air-conditioning equipment, elevators, machine tools, printing presses, and many others.

Other engineering specialties include agricultural engineers (12,000), biomedical engineers (3,000 and growing), ceramic engineers (12,000), metallurgical engineers (17,000), mining engineers (6,000 and growing), and petroleum engineers (20,000 and growing).

After two years with GE in Columbus Ohio, marathon runner Frank Csillag is a senior development engineer in the high-pressure research section where diamonds are made. The diamonds are developed mainly for manufacturing processes, such as drilling and grinding. Csillag is a Canadian who graduated from McGill University and then came to the U.S. to get a Ph.D. in engineering. He works in a lab until 5 or 6 p.m. each evening, but makes a point to be home nights and weekends with his wife, who is also his business partner, and his two-year-old daughter. Csillag and his wife have started a small manufacturing business in the basement of their home, where they create and produce soap detergents. "It takes a long time to make senior project engineer," says Csillag, "but once you get there, the track is clear—department head to division head to group head (vice president) to president." It took some thought before Csillag could come up with something he didn't like about his job. But he wishes other people were more open to new ideas. He hates to spend his time figuring out the politics necessary to get a new idea into action. Csillag loves his work. He especially likes the versatility of his job and the challenge to pursue his own way of making better diamonds. He mostly works alone, but he enjoys having other engineers working in the same lab with him on their own projects.

What Education and Skills Will I Need?

High school: Preparation for college, with an emphasis on science, mathematics, and computer science.

College: Major in engineering at one of the 240 colleges and universities. Specialize in aerospace, agricultural, biomedical, ceramic, chemical, civil, electrical, industrial, mechanical, metallurgical, mining, nuclear, or petroleum engineering. Some specialties such as nuclear engineering are available only on the graduate level.

Personal skills: Ability to think analytically, capacity for detail, and ability to work as a team member are necessary skills.

How Many Engineers Are There and Where Do They Work?

Engineering is the largest profession for men—99 percent of the 1.2 million engineers are men. Half of the engineers are employed by manufacturing industries; one-fourth are in construction, public utilities, and building services; and the remainder are with the government and with educational institutions.

$ $ $ $ $

In 1981, engineers with a bachelor's degree started at $22,900 a year. Master's degree graduates started at $25,500 a year, and experienced engineers doubled that salary. In 1980, average *starting* salaries for engineers, by branch, were:

Branch	Salary	Number Employed
Petroleum	$23,844	18,000
Chemical	$21,612	55,000
Mining	$20,808	6,000
Metallurgical	$20,712	15,000
Mechanical	$20,436	213,000
Electrical	$20,280	325,000
Industrial	$19,860	115,000
Aeronautical	$19,776	68,000
Civil	$18,648	165,000

What Is the Job Future?

The opportunities in engineering will continue to be excellent through the 1980s. Engineering students, who made up about 7 percent of the total number of college graduates in 1980, received 65 percent of the reported job offers. Many jobs will be open in developing new sources of energy and in solving environmental pollution problems.

RELATED CAREERS

environmental scientist
physical scientist
mathematician
architect

WHERE CAN I GET MORE INFORMATION?

Professional group
Engineers' Council for Professional Development
345 East 47 Street
New York, NY 10017

Trade journals
Chemical Engineer
McGraw-Hill Publications Company
1221 Avenue of the Americas
New York, NY 10019

Civil Engineering
345 East 47 Street
New York, NY 10017

ENVIRONMENTAL SCIENTIST

Geologists, geophysicists, meteorologists, and oceanographers study the earth's land, water, interior, and atmosphere, and the environment in space. They preserve our natural resources and control pollution.

What's It Like to Be an Environmental Scientist?

"The environmental sciences," writes a U.S. Geological Survey geologist, "share many methods with other fields of science—the collection of evidence leading to new conclusions, the application of all available techniques to test a hypothesis, and the thrill of discovery. In addition, they have certain satisfactions peculiar to themselves—the immediacy of using the earth as a laboratory, the healthful exercise of field work, and the unusual perspective one derives from dealing familiarly with the immensity of geological time." Geologists study the structure, composition, and history of the earth's crust. They spend a lot of time in the field studying rock cores and cuttings from deep holes drilled into the earth and examining rocks, minerals, and fossils near the surface of the earth. They locate oil, coal, and other minerals crucial to our scarce energy supply.

Geophysicists study the size and shape, interior, surface, and atmosphere of the earth, the land and bodies of water on its surface and underground, and the atmosphere surrounding it. They work mostly for oil and gas companies, often using satellites to conduct tests from outer space and computers to collect and analyze data.

Meterologists study the air that surrounds the earth, including the weather. Besides weather forecasting, they work to understand and solve air pollution problems.

Oceanographers study the ocean—its characteristics, movements, plant life, and animal life. Aquaculture is an industry for the 1980s, where oceanographers will be in high demand to get fish, food, and energy from a much needed new resource.

What Education and Skills Will I Need?

High school: Preparation for college, with an emphasis on the physical sciences, mathematics, life sciences, and computer science.

College: Major in any environmental science or related science to prepare for graduate work, which is necessary for any job in the sciences. A Ph.D. is required for a career in science, and a master's degree for a beginning job in research or high school teaching.

Personal skills: Curiosity to do new research, an analytical mind, and physical stamina for outdoor life are necessary skills.

How Many Environmental Scientists Are There and Where Do They Work?

There are 34,000 geologists, 12,000 geophysicists, 4,000 meteorologists, and 2,800 oceanographers. About 90 percent are men. Most environmental scientists work for private industry, oil and gas producers in the Southwest, agencies of the federal government, and in teaching.

$ $ $ $ $

In 1980, beginners with a master's degree started at $24,600 a year in private industry. The average salary for experienced oceanographers with the federal government was about $29,800 a year.

What Is the Job Future?

Oceanography will be a major industry in the 1980s. Opportunities will abound for the creative scientist in solving food problems, in solving energy problems by "growing oil" in the sea, in mining minerals, and in new directions as yet undiscovered as the ocean becomes "settled." Jobs in oceanography will continue to be competitive through the 1980s as the number of graduates exceeds the number of jobs. Chances for work in meteorology will be fair, but chances for work in geology and geophysics will be better because of the need to locate and recover oil and other minerals.

RELATED CAREERS

all environmental science and engineering careers

WHERE CAN I GET MORE INFORMATION?

Professional groups

American Geological Institute
5205 Leesburg Pike
Falls Church, VA 22041

American Geophysical Union
2000 Florida Avenue, NW
Washington, D.C. 20009

American Meteorological Society
45 Beacon Street
Boston, MA 02108

Office of Sea Grant
National Oceanic and Atmospheric Administration
Rockville, MD 20852

Trade journals

Sea Frontiers
10 Rickenbacker Causeway
Virginia Key, FL 33149

Rock and Minerals
Box 29
Peekskill, NY 10566

FOOD SCIENTIST

Investigates the chemical, physical, and biological nature of food for the processing industry.

What's It Like to Be a Food Scientist?

"The food business is going to be in the 1980s what the oil business was in the 1970s," predicts 70-year-old John Jacobson, Sr., head of Idle Wild Foods, a family-owned beef-packing business in Liberal, Kansas. Food scientists, sometimes called food technologists, study the structure and composition of food and their changes during processing or storage. They check raw ingredients to note freshness, maturity, or suitability for processing. Food scientists in the frozen food industry work to ensure that each new food product retains its characteristics and nutritive value during processing or storage. They determine the various enzymes that are inactive after the product has been processed so that the food does not lose its flavor during storage. Food scientists from Iowa Beef Processors have revolutionized the methods to process and finish beef. Their new technology that produces quality meat at much lower processing costs has forced most other beef packers out of the business.

What Education and Skills Will I Need?

High school: A college preparatory course, with a strong program in mathematics, biology, chemistry, and computer science.

College: A bachelor's degree in one of the 40 approved majors in food science, chemistry, or biology. A master's degree is required for management jobs in food science.

Personal skills: An analytical mind and an ability and interest to work with technical details are necessary.

How Many Food Scientists Are There and Where Do They Work?

Ninety percent of the 15,000 food scientists are men. Food scientists are employed in all parts of the food industry, and most of them work in California, Illinois, New York, Pennsylvania, Texas, Ohio, New Jersey, Wisconsin, Michigan, and Iowa.

$ $ $ $ $

In 1980, experienced food scientists earned an average of $29,500 a year. With 11 to 15 years of experience, they averaged $32,000 a year.

What Is the Job Future?

Work opportunities will be slow through the 1980s because of the slow growth rate of food processing industries. Jobs will increase if the food industry responds to the need for a wholesome and economical food supply in the world. Research could produce new foods from modifications of rice and soybeans. For example, from vegetable proteins food scientists may create "meat" products that resemble beef, pork, and chicken.

RELATED CAREERS

chemist
environmental scientist
engineer

WHERE CAN I GET MORE INFORMATION?

Professional group
The Institute of Food Technologists
221 North LaSalle Street, Suite 2120
Chicago, IL 60601

Trade journal
Quick Frozen Foods
Cahner Publishing Co.
205 East 42 Street
New York, NY 10017

MATHEMATICIAN

Creates new mathematical theories, and solves scientific, managerial, engineering, and social problems in mathematical terms.

What's It Like to Be a Mathematician?

Delbert O. Martin, a mathematician for GE and married with two elementary school children, spends half of his time learning or being creative. "This means," says Martin, "I apply mathematics to the solution of problems that cover econometrics and financial analysis. Also included are quality control analysis, which involves a great deal of statistics and probability application, and a lot of consulting with computer and engineering people who need mathematics input for their work. The remaining half of my time is spent in diverse duties such as report writing, seminars, workshops, teaching, using computers, and making presentations to management." Lunchtime for Martin is usually one hour of chess or bridge with friends at work. Several employees bring their own lunch and make their own place for relaxation. He rarely works overtime, but when he does it's usually to run a crisis problem on a computer. He and other mathematicians often take company or university postgraduate courses at night. Martin urges high school students to be persistent. He says, "Don't take the first failure seriously. I had to take elementary calculus three times before I passed it! Don't overlook the small colleges, and don't think you are born with math ability—everyone has to learn it. I like being a mathematician because my work is exciting, challenging, and creative. I like a forty-hour work week in a major corporation because that leaves me plenty of time for my two kids."

What Education and Skills Will I Need?

High school: Preparation for college, with emphasis in mathematics and computer science. Be sure that you elect fourth-year and advanced-placement mathematics in high school.

College: Major in mathematics, or in a related field with a minor in mathematics, to prepare for an advanced degree in mathematics, which is necessary for research and university teaching jobs.

Personal skills: Good reasoning ability, persistence, and ability to apply basic principles to new types of problems are necessary.

How Many Mathematicians Are There and Where Do They Work?

There are 40,000 mathematicians and three-fourths of them work in colleges and universities. Other mathematicians are employed by private industry, such as electrical, aerospace, and manufacturing companies, or are employed by the government. In addition, there are 26,500 statisticians, mostly in private industry.

$ $ $ $ $

In 1980, college graduates started at $17,700 a year with private industries, and master's degree graduates started at $20,200 a year. Colleges and government pay slightly less. In 1980, average salaries for all mathematicians in the federal government was $30,100 a year.

What Is the Job Future?

Jobs will be competitive for academic mathematicians through the 1980s, but related mathematics jobs are expected to increase. The growth in computer, engineering, and technical jobs will result in the use of many more mathematicians and statisticians. Applied rather than theoretical mathematicians will have the best chances for work.

RELATED CAREERS

computer programmer
systems analyst
actuary
statistician

WHERE CAN I GET MORE INFORMATION?

Professional groups

American Mathematical Society
P.O. Box 6248
Providence, RI 02940

American Statistical Association
806 15th Street, NW
Washington, D.C. 20005

Trade journal

Mathematics Magazine
MMA
1225 Connecticut Avenue, NW
Washington, D.C. 20036

PHYSICIST

Describes in mathematical terms the fundamental forces and laws of nature, and the interaction of matter and energy.

What's It Like to Be a Physicist?

Physicists develop theories that describe in mathematical terms the basic forces and laws of nature, such as gravity, electromagnetism, and nuclear interaction. Most work in research and development for private industry and the government, and they often specialize in areas such as nuclear energy, electronics, communications, aerospace, or medical instrumentation. Physicist Dr. Robert S. Wright, married with one young child, works on the west coast for a company that is engineering-oriented. The company uses applied physics to develop transistors used in electronic equipment, hearing aids, and missile guidance systems. Wright finds his job very creative; he often works alone investigating new possibilities for applied physics. His family provides a good change from his isolated workstyle.

What Education and Skills Will I Need?

High school: Preparation for college, with as much mathematics and computer science as possible.

College: Major in physics or mathematics in college to prepare for graduate school. A career in physics requires a Ph.D. degree with computer skills.

Personal skills: Mathematical ability, an inquisitive mind, and imagination are needed to be a physicist.

How Many Physicists Are There and Where Do They Work?

There are 37,000 physicists. Half of them are employed by private industry, primarily in companies that manufacture electrical, aircraft and missile, and scientific instruments; most of the other half are in colleges and universities, and some are with the government. More than one-third of all physicists work in three states—California, New York, and Massachusetts.

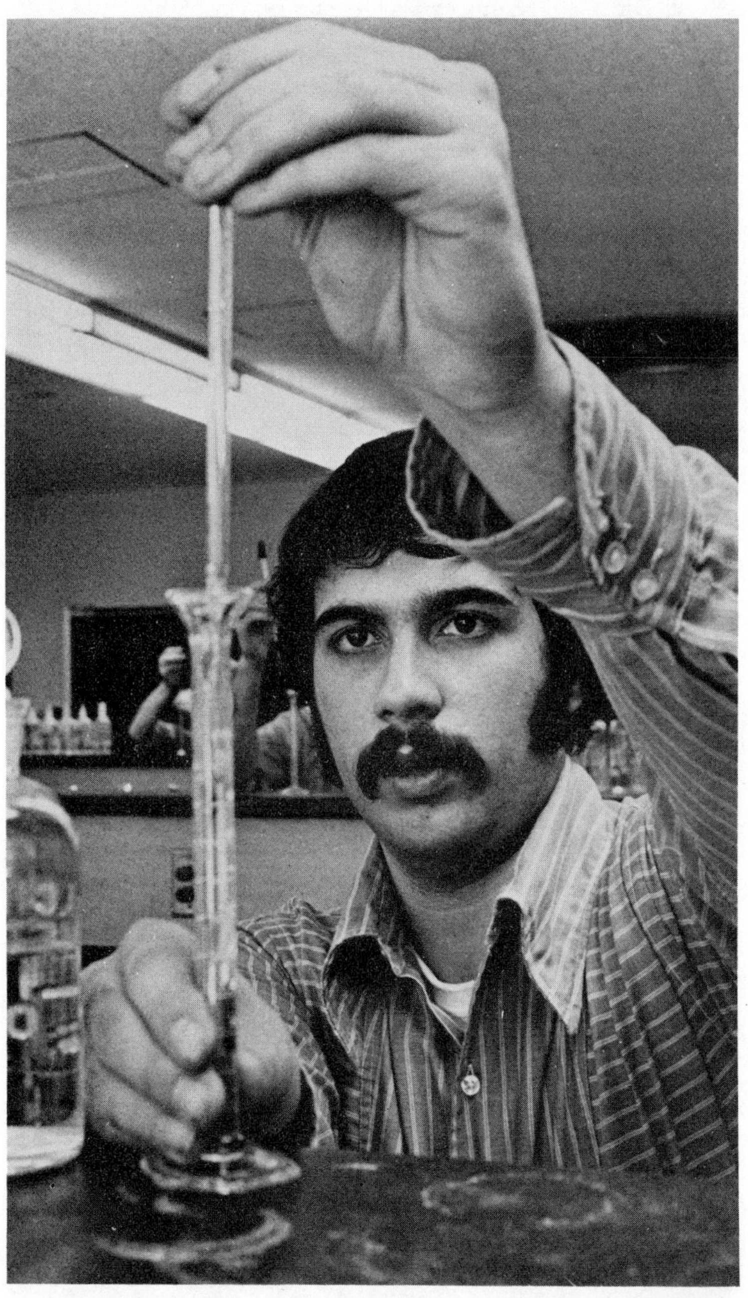

PHYSICIST

$ $ $ $ $

In 1980, beginning physicists in private industry with a master's degree started at $21,500 a year and with a Ph.D. degree at $27,300 a year. Average salary for all physicists in the federal government in 1980 was $34,700.

What Is the Job Future?

Opportunities for physicists are expected to be good through the 1980s. A bachelor's degree in physics qualifies you for jobs in engineering and computer science.

RELATED CAREERS

astronomer
chemist
geologist
engineer
mathematician

WHERE CAN I GET MORE INFORMATION?

Professional group
American Institute of Physics
335 East 45 Street
New York, NY 10017

Trade journal
Physics Today
American Institute of Physics
335 East 45 Street
New York, NY 10017

Clergy
Extension Service Worker
Home Economist
Recreation Worker
Rehabilitation Counselor
Social Worker

About these careers Over 732,000 social service jobs are represented in this career cluster. Like those in education, social service jobs require more education for less pay than any other fields of work. Concern for people, not desire for money, are needed to be happy in this career. Patience, tact, sensitivity, and compassion are necessary personal qualities.

In social service careers, there are a great variety of settings and tasks. Depending on their specific occupation, workers may advise consumers on how to get the most for their money; help people with disabilities to achieve satisfactory lifestyles; provide religious services; counsel people having problems in their job, home, school, or social relationships; or treat people with emotional problems.

Although social services are provided in many different settings, people in these careers require many of the same skills. In general, a knowledge of the field is gained through a college degree. One to three years of graduate work in a professional school are required for many social service careers, such as counseling, clergy, and social work.

Beginning rehabilitation counselors and social workers who have limited experience are assigned the less difficult cases. As they gain experience, their caseloads are increased and they are assigned clients with more complex problems. After getting experience and more graduate education, rehabilitation counselors and social workers may advance to supervisory positions or top administrative jobs.

After a few years of experience, recreation leaders may become supervisors. Although promotions to administrative jobs may be easier with graduate training, advancement is still possible through a combination of education and experience.

Social service jobs usually involve irregular hours, because the workers provide a wide range of services to people in many circumstances. For example, the clergy must go to people whenever they are in crisis, as well as visit regularly. Those in extension work frequently serve longer hours than they might in other jobs because they must be available for evening lectures and demonstrations. Recreation workers can expect night work and irregular hours, since they often have to work while others are enjoying leisure time.

Social service jobs often depend on government spending, because so many of the programs are tied to federal budgets. When money is tight and budgets are cut, the job situation becomes a very tough one.

CLERGY

Religious leaders within the Jewish, Roman Catholic, and Protestant religious institutions.

What's It Like to Be a Member of the Clergy?

Young people who choose to enter the ministry, priesthood, or rabbinate do so mainly because they have a strong religious faith and a desire to help others. Deciding on a career in the clergy involves considerations different from other career choices. In addition to the clergy who serve in congregations and parishes, there are teachers and administrators in education; chaplains in the military, prisons, hospitals, and on college campuses; and missionaries and those who serve in social welfare agencies. Catholic priest Sean McManus, school prefect and parish priest in Roxbury, Massachusetts, likes best being helpful to students by being interested in their human struggles. "It makes people feel good to have a priest interested in their lives." He doesn't like the stereotype of a priest and the authority role he is always put in. Like all religious priests, McManus has taken the vow of poverty. He likes the simple lifestyle; he lives in common with the other priests and brothers.

Protestant ministers lead their congregations in worship services and administer the rites of baptism, confirmation, and Holy Communion. They prepare and deliver sermons, and give religious instruction to new members of the church.

Rabbis are the spiritual leaders of their congregations, and teachers and interpreters of Jewish law and tradition. They conduct religious services and deliver sermons on the Sabbath and on Jewish holidays. Rabbis serve either Orthodox, Conservative, or Reform congregations. The congregations differ in the extent to which they follow the traditional form of worship, for example, in wearing head coverings, in using Hebrew as the language of prayer, or in using music and a choir.

Roman Catholic priests attend to the spiritual, pastoral, moral, and educational needs of the members of their church. Their duties include presiding at liturgical functions, delivering sermons, hearing confessions, administering the Sacraments, and conducting funeral services. There are two main classifications of priests—diocesan (secular) and religious. Diocesan priests generally work as individuals in parishes assigned to them by the bishop of their diocese. Religious priests generally work as part of a religious order, such as Jesuits, Dominicans, or Franciscans. They engage in specialized work assigned to them by superiors in their order.

All clergy conduct weddings and funeral services, visit the sick, help the poor, comfort the bereaved, supervise religious education programs, engage in interfaith activities, and involve themselves in community affairs. Clergy serving smaller churches or synagogues usually work on a personal basis with their parishioners. Those serving large congregations have greater administrative responsibilities. They spend a lot of time working with committees, church officers, and staff, besides performing many community duties. They often have one or more associates who share specific aspects of the ministry, and who help them meet the individual needs of the parishioners.

What Education and Skills Will I Need?

High school: Preparation for a strong liberal arts college program.

College: Major in religion, or theology, or any related field to do with understanding people, as preparation for a master's degree in divinity for Protestants, a three-year to five-year seminary program for Jews, and a four-year seminary program for Catholics.

Personal skills: Religious careers require a deep conviction in the religious and spiritual needs of people, and the ability to fulfill those personal needs through the spiritual leadership of others.

How Many Clergy Are There and Where Do They Work?

There are 230,000 Protestant ministers serving 72 million people. About 1,550 Orthodox, 1,550 Conservative, and 1,110 Reform rabbis serve 6 million people. There are 58,000 priests serving nearly 49 million people. Other than five percent of the Protestant ministers, and a very few rabbis, virtually all clergy are white men.

$ $ $ $ $

In 1980 average salary for Protestant ministers was about $15,000 a year; $20,000 to $50,000 for rabbis; and a stipend of $2,000 to $6,000 plus all maintenance expenses for priests, who take a vow of poverty.

What Is the Job Future?

Protestant and Jewish jobs will continue to be competitive through the 1980s, as church enrollments decrease. Many theological graduates will go into related social agency and teaching jobs. Catholic priests are in demand because of a sharp drop in seminary enrollments, and chances for a career in the priesthood will be plentiful.

RELATED CAREERS

social worker
counselor
chaplain
missionary

WHERE CAN I GET MORE INFORMATION?

Professional groups

Your local church or synagogue can offer you names and addresses of the headquarters of your religious group for career information.

B'Nai B'Rith Career and Counseling Services
1640 Rhode Island Avenue, NW
Washington, D.C. 20036 (Jewish)

Executive Director, National Conference
Religious Vocation Directors of Men
22 West Monroe Street
Chicago, IL 60608 (Catholic)

National Council of Churches
475 Riverside Drive
New York, NY 10027 (Protestant)

Trade journals

Christian Century
407 South Dearborn Street
Chicago, IL 60605 (Protestant)

Commentary
165 East 56 Street
New York, NY 10022 (Jewish)

Commonweal
232 Madison Avenue
New York, NY 10016 (Catholic)

EXTENSION SERVICE WORKER

Helps rural families solve their farm and home problems and aids in community improvement.

What's It Like to Be an Extension Service Worker?

County extension service workers help farmers produce higher-quality crops and livestock more efficiently. They help farm youth with recreation, health, leadership, and educational decisions. They work with homemakers on nutrition and enjoyment in family living. Mass media are used often for special newsletters, radio programs, and television programs for farm people. Winston Way, married with three grown children, is an extension service worker in Vermont. He gives about 150 speaking engagements a year for farm families, and also does television shows on home gardens. "My slant is always education for everything I do," says Way. Whether he's working on field crops, fertilizer, environment, food supply, or pollution, he is always trying to teach the farm family new alternatives for doing things.

What Education and Skills Will I Need?

High school: Preparation for college. A college degree is required.

College: Specialize in agriculture, family development, sociology, psychology, veterinary medicine, engineering, business, economics, or public administration.

Personal skills: Extension service workers should have a specialty, an ability to work with people, and a strong interest in farm life.

How Many Extension Service Workers Are There and Where Do They Work?

There are 14,000 extension service workers who manage county programs and workers in all rural parts of the U.S., as well as in the state capital of each state.

$ $ $ $ $

Extension service workers earn the same as other college graduates in government jobs, averaging $20,000 a year in 1980.

What Is the Job Future?

Job opportunities will be few through the 1980s. Cuts in federal spending and focus on cities will slow down job growth in rural areas.

RELATED CAREERS

dietitian	home economist
counselor	agricultural chemical salesperson

WHERE CAN I GET MORE INFORMATION?

Professional group
County Extension Office, Personnel Division
U.S. Department of Agriculture
Hyattsville, MD 20782

Trade journal
Extension Service Review
U.S. Department of Agriculture
South Building, Room 5044
Washington, D.C. 20250

HOME ECONOMIST

Concerned with improving products, services, and practices that affect the comfort and well-being of the family.

What's It Like to Be a Home Economist?

Half of the home economists are secondary school teachers. Home economists also work in private industry to test products, prepare advertising materials, and plan and present radio and television programs. They study consumer needs and help manufacturers find useful and saleable products. Clothing and textile majors work for clothing and textile patterns companies, interior designers, and fabric manufacturers. Home economists work in extension services in adult education programs and 4-H clubs. Robert Tyzbir, a married professor of home economics with two young children, teaches nutrition, which involves the cultural, chemical, metabolic, and medical aspects of food. His special interest is in history and what we eat today. Tyzbir integrates his research with his family's nutritional needs, and uses the results as content in his advanced classes.

What Education and Skills Will I Need?

High school: Preparation for college, with emphasis on the sciences.

College: Major in home economics and specialize in any of the areas that interest you: child development, family relations, clothing and textiles, foods and nutrition, or institution management.

Personal skills: Home economists should be able to work with people from many incomes and cultural backgrounds, have the capacity for leadership, and have an interest in changing roles within the family.

How Many Home Economists Are There and Where Do They Work?

There are 128,000 home economists, and very few are men. There are 75,000 teachers, 33,000 dietitians, 50,000 high school teachers, 7,000 college and university teachers, 5,800 extension service workers, and 5,000 workers in private industry. A growing number of men are entering this field, especially in college administration positions where the top money is.

$ $ $ $ $

In 1980, most beginning teachers in large secondary schools started at $11,500 a year. Extension service workers earned about the same, and workers in the federal government and private industry earned slightly more.

What Is the Job Future?

Chances for work in home economics are better than in most teaching jobs through the 1980s. Consumer education with computer skills will be in demand in business careers.

RELATED CAREERS

dietitian
food scientist
hotel-restaurant management

WHERE CAN I GET MORE INFORMATION?

Professional group
American Home Economics Association
2010 Massachusetts Avenue, NW
Washington, D.C. 20036

Trade journal
What's New in Home Economics
Donnelley, Dun, and Bradstreet
466 Lexington Avenue
New York, NY 10017

RECREATION WORKER

Helps people develop good physical and mental health through recreation and group activity within an organization

What's It Like to Be a Recreation Worker?

Recreation workers organize activities for all ages and interests at community centers, churches, hospitals, camps, and playgrounds. The major youth agencies are the Boy Scouts, YMCA, 4-H Clubs, and American Youth Hostels. These organizations help people to use and enjoy their leisure time constructively in physical, social, and cultural programs. Recreation directors lead classes and discussions, teach skills, take charge of hikes and trips, and direct programs and camps. They operate recreational facilities and study recreational needs of individuals and communities. Garcia Rodriguez and his wife, Pam, camp directors of a coed camp for sailing, have developed a year-round business promoting, running, and operating their camp for teenagers. They each worked for several agencies before they decided to go into business together. Garcia, a physical education major, taught school in the winter and sailing in the summer before he and his wife decided to go into the camping business.

What Education and Skills Will I Need?

High school: Preparation for community college or four-year college.

College: Half of the professional recreation workers are college graduates. The community-college graduate also has employment opportunities in recreation work. A major in physical education, recreation, or social sciences and a master's degree are necessary for many administration jobs.

Personal skills: Skill in sports, music, and crafts; creativity and enthusiasm about activities; and good judgment are necessary for success in recreation.

How Many Recreation Workers Are There and Where Do They Work?

Over half of the 135,000 full-time recreation workers are men. In addition, there are 100,000 part-time workers employed

RECREATION WORKER

in the summer at parks, camps, and other outdoor recreation sites. The majority of the full-time recreation workers work for local government and volunteer agencies, religious organizations, national parks, correctional institutions, and the Armed Forces.

$ $ $ $ $

In 1980, beginners with a college degree made $11,500 a year. Community supervisors of recreation averaged $17,000 a year.

What Is the Job Future?

Recreation jobs are competitive. The best opportunities will be in therapeutic recreation and private and commercial recreation. Part-time opportunities are unlimited. Many new programs for retired people will create more jobs. The best chances for employment will go to those with experience from summer work.

RELATED CAREERS

club manager
town guide
physical education teacher
camp director
physical therapist

WHERE CAN I GET MORE INFORMATION?

Professional group
National Recreation and Park Association
3101 Park Central Drive
Arlington, VA 22302

Trade journal
Recreation Management
20 North Wacker Drive
Chicago, IL 60606

REHABILITATION COUNSELOR

Helps disabled persons make a satisfactory occupational adjustment, mainly through counseling them.

What's It Like to Be a Rehabilitation Counselor?

Rehabilitation counselors interview people with disabilities to learn about their abilities and interests. Walter Rutherford, rehabilitation counselor in a small city, says, "Each day I work out a plan of rehabilitation after consulting with the person's social worker and medical doctor, and sometimes with their family. I work with 75 to 100 people in groups, and sometimes individually in the home if a person is severely disabled." Alcoholics, the mentally ill, and the retarded are the main groups of people counselors work with. "I keep in contact with my clients' employers and develop contacts with new employers who will hire the disabled," continues Rutherford. "The amount of direct counseling varies with each person, but I try to involve families and other agencies to help the clients, as they try to get back to work on a regular basis."

What Education and Skills Will I Need?

High school: Preparation for college, with emphasis on the social sciences.

College: Major in education, psychology, guidance, or sociology to prepare for graduate school. A master's degree in psychology, student personnel, vocational counseling, or rehabilitation counseling is usually required.

Personal skills: Ability to accept responsibility, to work independently, and to motivate others are all necessary to be successful in rehabilitation.

How Many Rehabilitation Counselors Are There and Where Do They Work?

Sixty-six percent of the 25,000 rehabilitation counselors are men. One-third of them are employed by state or local rehabilitation agencies. The rest work in hospitals, labor unions, insurance companies, and sheltered workshops.

$ $ $ $ $

In 1980, the average starting salary for counselors in state agencies was $13,300 a year. Veterans Administration hospitals paid slightly more. Experienced counselors in the federal government averaged $23,400 a year.

What Is the Job Future?

Counselors with a master's degree are expected to have fair job opportunities through the 1980s. Services are needed but federal spending for these jobs is low.

RELATED CAREERS

counselor
psychologist
social worker

WHERE CAN I GET MORE INFORMATION?

Professional group
American Rehabilitation Counseling Association
Two Skyline Place
5203 Leesburg Pike, Suite 400
Falls Church, VA 22041

Trade journal
Rehabilitation Record
Government Printing Office
Washington, D.C. 20402

SOCIAL WORKER

Helps those individuals and families who cannot provide for themselves or solve their problems to use the government social services available to them.

What's It Like to Be a Social Worker?

Social workers plan and conduct activities for children, adolescents, and older people in settlement houses, hospitals, and correctional institutions. *Family service workers* try to strengthen family life and improve its functioning. *Child-welfare workers* work to improve physical and emotional well-being of deprived and troubled children. They advise parents on child care and work with the school social workers and community leaders. *School social workers* are employed in the public schools; *medical social workers* work in hospitals; and *psychiatric social workers* work in mental health centers and clinics. Cy Abdelnour, 30-year-old social worker for a state agency, prefers working with children. He feels that chances are better for changes in attitudes and behavior in a child's life than in an adult's. Abdelnour works with children in school, in courts, and in child centers. His lunch is usually with a child at the nearest McDonald's. He often visits children at their homes after school, and his evenings include taking clients to sports events and school plays.

What Education and Skills Will I Need?

High school: Preparation for college, with as broad an education as possible.

College: Major in one of the social sciences to prepare for graduate school, or take a bachelor's degree in social work (BSW). A master's degree is required to be a professional member of the National Association of Social Workers.

Personal skills: To be happy in social work, you must be sensitive to others, as objective as possible, and have a basic concern for people and their problems.

How Many Social Workers Are There and Where Do They Work?

There are 345,000 social workers, and 100,000 of them are men. Two-thirds are employed by state, county, and city government agencies, while the others work in private agencies. The administrative jobs in social work are increasingly being held by men, even though most social workers are women.

$ $ $ $ $

In 1980, the average starting salary for a caseworker with a bachelor's degree was $12,000 a year. A caseworker with a master's degree and one year's experience earned $16,300 a year. In 1981, the federal government started social workers with a master's degree at $18,585 a year.

What Is the Job Future?

Fair job opportunities for full-time, part-time, and temporary work will continue through the 1980s. The number of graduates is increasing, however, and in some parts of the country, the jobs are very competitive. Cuts in federal spending for social programs will severely limit job opportunities.

RELATED CAREERS

clergy
psychologist
counselor

WHERE CAN I GET MORE INFORMATION?

Professional groups
National Association of Social Workers
1425 H Street, NW, Suite 600
Washington, D.C. 20005

Social Work Vocational Bureau
386 Park Avenue South
New York, NY 10016

Trade journal
Social Work
National Association of Social Workers
1425 H Street, NW, Suite 600
Washington, D.C. 20005

SOCIAL SCIENCE

Anthropologist
Economist
Geographer
Historian
Political Scientist
Psychologist
Sociologist

About these careers *Social science is a career field where a Ph.D. is needed for many entrance-level positions and for almost all of the top jobs. Other than economists, most social scientists work in colleges and universities where the job market for Ph.D.s has crashed. By 1985, there will be 40,000 more Ph.D.s in social science than job openings.*

There are 228,000 jobs represented in the basic social sciences described in this career cluster. Overlapping among basic social science fields—and the sometimes hazy distinction between social science and related fields such as business administration, foreign service work, and high school teaching—makes it difficult to determine the exact size of each profession. Economists, however, are the largest social science group, and anthropologists are the smallest.

The trend in some industries is to hire increasing numbers of social science majors as trainees for administrative and executive positions. Research councils and other nonprofit organizations provide an important source of employment for economists, political scientists, and sociologists.

Every liberal arts college in the country offers a major in most of the social sciences. The choice of a graduate school is important for people who want to become social scientists. Students interested in research should select schools that emphasize training in research, statistics, and computers. Opportunities to gain practical experience in research work also may be available. Professors and heads of social science departments often help in the placement of graduates.

Working conditions in the social sciences are very good, because most colleges provide sabbatical leaves of absence, life and health insurance, and retirement plans. Working hours are generally flexible, with few teaching hours when a professor must actually "be there." Professors with tenure have a low-stress job with prestige. The biggest problem is finding employment. Clinical and counseling psychologists often work in the evenings, since their patients are sometimes unable to leave their jobs or school during the day.

Social science is one of the most overcrowded career clusters. If social science is where you want to be, prepare for applied science by acquiring computer and management skills.

ANTHROPOLOGIST

Studies people—their origins, physical characteristics, customs, languages, traditions, material possessions, structured social relationships, and value systems.

What's It Like to Be an Anthropologist?

Anthropologists usually specialize in cultural anthropology (sometimes called ethnology), archeology, linguistics, and physical anthropology. *Ethnologists* may spend long periods (up to two years) living in tribal groups to learn a people's way of life. In recent years, their studies have included complex urban societies. *Archeologists* dig for past civilizations. They excavate and study the remains of homes, tools, ornaments, and evidence of activity, in order to reconstruct the people's history and customs. *Linguists* scientifically study the sounds and structures of languages and the relationship between language and people's behavior. *Physical anthroplogists* study human evolution by comparing the physical characteristics of different races or groups of people. Related to these basic areas of study are subfields of applied, urban, and medical anthropology. Anthropologist Dr. William E. Mitchell, specialist in ethnology, took his family, including two preschool children, to the bush of New Guinea for two years. Mitchell encourages young people to be an anthroplogist if they "have an insatiable curiosity about people and the patience and tact to study first-hand the different ways—often strange to us—that human groups have arranged to live their lives. What delights me most about being an anthropologist," says Mitchell, "is the fact that the problems are so immense and the factors so complex for understanding human behavior that it will always elude my grasp. I may sometimes be frustrated but *never* bored with my work."

What Education and Skills Will I Need?

High school: Strong college preparatory course to prepare for a competitive liberal arts college program.

College: Liberal arts degree to prepare for graduate work. Most anthropologists major in a social science, although you don't have to be an anthropology major in your undergraduate work. A Ph.D. in anthropology is required for a professional career in a university or in research.

ANTHROPOLOGIST

Personal skills: Reading, research, and writing skills are essential, as well as an interest in detail and an ability to work independently.

How Many Anthropologists Are There and Where Do They Work?

There are 7,200 anthropologists and almost all of them work in colleges and universities. A few are employed by the federal government, by museums, and in related social science jobs.

$ $ $ $ $

In 1980, starting salaries in college teaching for beginners with a Ph.D. were from $15,600 to $19,500 a year. Experienced anthropologists may earn up to twice that amount. Many anthropologists supplement their teaching salaries with grants for research in the summer, field trips for students, and summer-school teaching.

What Is the Job Future?

As college enrollments decline, there will be little chance for a college teaching job through the 1980s. Very limited opportunities will be available in museums, research programs, and public health programs. There are many more Ph.D.s in anthropology than jobs.

RELATED CAREERS

sociologist   reporter
psychologist   community planner

WHERE CAN I GET MORE INFORMATION?

Professional group
American Anthropological Association
1703 New Hampshire Avenue, NW
Washington, D.C. 20009

Trade journal
Anthropology Newsletter
American Anthropological Association
1703 New Hampshire Avenue, NW
Washington, D.C. 20009

ECONOMIST

Studies how goods and services are produced, distributed, and consumed.

What's It Like to Be an Economist?

An economist deals with the relationship between supply and demand for goods and services. Some work with specific fields, such as control of inflation, prevention of depression, and development of farm, wage, and tax policies. Others develop theories to explain causes of employment and unemployment, international trade influences, and world economic conditions. Roger McIntosh, who just got a master's degree from a western university, is a trainee for a major insurance company. He works with the actuaries and sales administrators in making company policy. "Economists in business," says McIntosh, "provide management with information to make decisions on the marketing and pricing of company products; the effect of government policies on business or trade; or the advisability of adding new lines of merchandise, opening new branch operations, or otherwise expanding the company's business."

What Education and Skills Will I Need?

High school: Preparation for a liberal arts program in college, with as strong a program as is offered in high school.

College: Major in economics, or a related social science, or mathematics with computer science and statistics to prepare for an advanced degree in economics. A Ph.D. is required for the top teaching or research jobs in an economics career.

Personal skills: Ability and interest in detailed accurate research is needed. Most economists must be able to express themselves well in writing.

How Many Economists Are There and Where Do They Work?

Of the 44,000 economists, 90 percent are men. Three-quarters work in private industry and research agencies, one-fifth teach in colleges, and one-sixth are employed by the government. The largest number of economists are employed in New York and Washington.

$ $ $ $ $

In 1980, new graduates with a Ph.D. degree started from $12,300 to $19,300 a year. Economists in colleges receive the same pay as other professors. The average salary of economists in the private sector was $38,000 a year in 1980.

What Is the Job Future?

Jobs will be very competitive through the 1980s for economists. The best chances for work will be with business and consulting firms for economists trained in econometrics and statistics.

RELATED CAREERS

financial analyst
bank officer
accountant
actuary
research analyst

WHERE CAN I GET MORE INFORMATION?

Professional group
American Economic Association
1313 21st Avenue South
Nashville, TN 37212

Trade journal
Job Openings for Economists
American Economic Association
1313 21st Avenue South
Nashville, TN 37212

GEOGRAPHER

Studies the physical characteristics of the earth—its terrain, minerals, soils, water, vegetation, and climate.

What's It Like to Be a Geographer?

Geographers analyze maps and aerial photographs, and also construct maps, graphs, and diagrams. They analyze the distribution and structure of political organizations, transportation systems, and marketing systems. Mike Taupier, a 30-year-old graduate student in geography, is looking for a job in the ecological sciences. "Geography," says Taupier, "isn't as popular as many other sciences and the job market is better. It fits into work with both physical and social sciences, and is often related to work in botany, geology, political science, and history." Many geographers have job titles such as cartographer, map analyst, or regional planner that describe their specialization. Others have titles that relate to their subject matter, such as photo-intelligence specialist or climatological analyst. Still others have titles such as community planner and market or business analyst.

What Education and Skills Will I Need?

High school: Preparation for college, with emphasis on all social and biological sciences.

College: Graduate work is required for a career in geography. There are about 56 U.S. universities offering a Ph.D. in geography.

Personal skills: Reading, studying, computing, and research skills are needed, along with an interest in working independently.

How Many Geographers Are There and Where Do They Work?

There are 15,000 geographers and 85 percent are men. Many of them teach in colleges; the remainder are with the government, primarily in the Departments of Defense and Interior.

$ $ $ $ $

In 1980, a master's degree graduate started with the federal government at $18,600 a year; a Ph.D. graduate started at $22,500 a year. Cartographers with the federal government averaged around $25,300 a year.

What Is the Job Future?

The outlook for work is better than for most Ph.D.s through the 1980s. Those with quantitative skills and training in cartography, satellite data interpretation, or planning should have the best prospects.

RELATED CAREERS

engineer
oceanographer
geologist

WHERE CAN I GET MORE INFORMATION?

Professional group
Association of American Geographers
1710 16th Street, NW
Washington, D.C. 20009

Trade journal
Annals
Association of American Geographers
1710 16th Street, NW
Washington, D.C. 20009

HISTORIAN

Studies the records of the past and analyzes events, institutions, ideas, and people.

What's It Like to Be an Historian?

Historians relate their knowledge of the past to current events, in an effort to explain the present. They may specialize in the history of a specific country or area, or a particular period of time, such as ancient, medieval, or modern. They also may specialize in the history of a field, such as economics, culture, the labor movement, art, or architecture. The number of specialities in history is constantly growing. Newer specialites are concerned with business archives, quantitative analysis, and the relationship between technological and other aspects of historical development. A growing number of historians now specialize in African, Latin American, Chinese, Asian, or Near Eastern history. For example, Harvey J. Spalding, a black Ph.D., majored in African history in college. He now works for a black historical society that is seeking new understandings about minorities in America. Other specialities include archivists, who are associated with museums, special libraries, and historical societies.

What Education and Skills Will I Need?

High school: Preparation for college, with a strong social science background.

College: Most historians major in history, with minors in government, economics, sociology, or anthropology. A doctorate is necessary for a career in college teaching and for better government jobs.

Personal skills: An interest in reading, studying, and research and the ability to write papers and reports are necessary for historians.

How Many Historians Are There and Where Do They Work?

There are 20,000 historians and 87 percent are men. Seventy percent of all historians work in colleges and universities, with others employed by the federal government, archives, libraries, museums, and historical societies.

$ $ $ $ $

In 1980, the average annual salary for a historian was $23,900. Museum curators averaged $28,300 a year.

What Is the Job Future?

Historians will find stiff competition in all employment opportunities through the 1980s. There are many more Ph.D.s in history than there are jobs for them. People with computer skills are expected to have the best chance for a job in business and research.

RELATED CAREERS

political scientist	sociologist
economist	journalist

WHERE CAN I GET MORE INFORMATION?

Professional group
American Historical Association
400 A Street, SE
Washington, D.C. 20003

Trade journal
American Heritage
551 Fifth Avenue
New York, NY 10017

POLITICAL SCIENTIST

Studies how political power is amassed and used.

What's It Like to Be a Political Scientist?

Most political scientists teach in colleges and universities, where they combine research, consultation, or administration with teaching. Many of them specialize in a general area of political science, including political theory, U.S. political institutions and processes, comparative political processes, or international relations. Joseph Mannelli is a graduate student in political science. He is married to a political scientist and they both plan to work together in research for a private firm to survey public opinion on political questions. They can also use their research skills to study proposed legislation for reference bureaus and congressional committees. Mannelli and Mannelli hope to eventually start their own legislative research service business.

What Education and Skills Will I Need?

High school: Preparation for college, with an emphasis on history, government, and the social sciences.

College: Major in political science or in a related major, such as government, history, or economics, to prepare for graduate work. Almost all political scientists have a master's degree for a beginning job, and a Ph.D. is required for a career in political science. Law school is an alternative to a Ph.D.

Personal skills: Political scientists must have an interest in details, be objective in their thinking, and have good oral and writing skills.

How Many Political Scientists Are There and Where Do They Work?

There are 15,000 political scientists and three-fourths teach in college. Others are employed by government agencies, political organizations, public interest groups, labor unions, and research institutes.

$ $ $ $ $

In 1981, political scientists with a master's degree started with the federal government at $18,600 a year. Intelligence specialists averaged $29,400 a year in 1980.

What Is the Job Future?

Employment opportunities are very competitive in college teaching, business, and government. A political science degree is helpful for a career in journalism, foreign affairs, law, or other related work. Well qualified economists with computer skills will find the best chances in applied fields.

RELATED CAREERS

politician
writer
lawyer
city manager

WHERE CAN I GET MORE INFORMATION?

Professional group
American Political Science Association
1527 New Hampshire Avenue, NW
Washington, D.C. 20036

Trade journal
Interplay
Walking Corporation
200 West 57 Street
New York, NY 10019

PSYCHOLOGIST

Studies the behavior of individuals and groups in order to understand and explain their actions.

What's It Like to Be a Psychologist?

A clinical psychologist working in a mental-health clinic spends most of his time testing clients with individual psychological tests and scoring the tests. He meets with the clinic team of social worker, psychiatrist, and educator to interpret the test scores and determine ways to help the individual. A psychologist often works with group-therapy classes of young parents, adolescents, children, or whatever group needs therapy in the particular community or agency. He has conferences with parents, community leaders, and educators about clients in the clinic, and tries to get all groups to make a joint effort toward helping a person in stress. Juan Chaurez, a school psychologist, also has a private practice in Los Angeles in partnership with his psychologist wife. She spends a lot of time visiting schools and clinics to build up a referral system for new clients. Chaurez spends his evenings and weekends specializing with his wife in the fastest growing market—marriage counseling.

What Education and Skills Will I Need?

High school: Preparation for college, with a science, computer science, and social science emphasis.

College: Most psychologists major in psychology, although some major in a related field such as sociology, anthropology, or education, and prepare for graduate work in psychology. A master's degree is required for most practical work in psychology, including school psychologist, psychologist in a government agency, and mental health work. A Ph.D. is required for research, college teaching jobs, and promotions in most jobs.

Personal skills: Sensitivity to others and a genuine interest in people are important for counseling. Research jobs require an interest in detail, accuracy, and writing skills.

How Many Psychologists Are There and Where Do They Work?

About half of the 106,000 psychologists are men. Almost half teach in colleges and universities. Hospitals, clinics, and other health facilities employ the second largest group. In addition, government, public schools, and private industry employ psychologists.

$ $ $ $ $

In 1980, the average annual salary for a psychologist with a doctoral degree was $26,000. Self-employed psychologists who do consulting work and see patients privately earned more. Ph.D.s in business and industry averaged $36,700 a year.

What Is the Job Future?

There will be 22,000 more Ph.D.s in psychology than jobs through 1985. However, there are some jobs, with the best opportunities in school psychology. University jobs will be most competitive.

RELATED CAREERS

psychiatrist
social worker
clergy
counselor

WHERE CAN I GET MORE INFORMATION?

Professional group
American Psychological Association
1200 17th Street, NW
Washington, D.C. 20036

Trade journal
Behavorial Science
Mental Health Research Institute
University of Michigan
Ann Arbor, MI 48104

SOCIOLOGIST

Studies the behavior and interaction of people in groups.

What's It Like to Be a Sociologist?

Sociologists learn how people are affected by their families, by their schools, and by their work. They provide professionals in the helping careers, such as social workers, educators, and nurses, with some idea of what makes people behave as they do. America has every kind of group of people, and the possibilities for research are limited only by a lack of imagination. Some sociologists study the causes of social problems such as crime or poverty, the pattern of family relations, or the different patterns of living in communities of varying types and sizes. Increasingly, sociologists are working in prison systems, education, industrial public relations, and regional and community planning.

What Education and Skills Will I Need?

High school: Preparation for college, with a strong academic program and computer skills.

College: Major in any social science and prepare for graduate work in sociology. A Ph.D. is required for a career in sociology.

Personal skills: Study and research skills are crucial for the sociologist, as are communication skills, especially writing.

How Many Sociologists Are There and Where Do They Work?

There are 21,000 sociologists and two-thirds are employed by colleges and universities, ten percent by government agencies, and the remainder by private industry and welfare agencies.

$ $ $ $ $

In 1980, the average annual salary for a social scientist with a doctorate was $26,000. Industry paid $33,600 a year, the federal government $34,400 a year, and education $25,600 a year.

What Is the Job Future?

College jobs are very competitive, as there will be thousands of Ph.D.s in sociology without openings through the 1980s.

RELATED CAREERS

anthropologist	political scientist
historian	community planner

WHERE CAN I GET MORE INFORMATION?

Professional group
American Sociological Association
1772 N Street, NW
Washington, D.C. 20036

Trade journal
Society
Rutgers, The State University, Box A
New Brunswick, NJ 08903

TRANSPORTATION

Airline Pilot
Air Traffic Controller
Flight Attendant
Merchant Marine Officer

About these careers *There are 4.7 million workers in transportation and public utilities, and 7.4 percent, or 340,000, of them are college graduates. There are 184,000 transportation jobs represented by the careers described in this cluster.*

Even though airline pilots are usually college graduates, most get their flight training in the military. Air traffic controllers come from many college backgrounds, flight attendants usually have two years of college, and merchant marine officers are trained at the United States Merchant Marine Academy at Kings Point, New York, or at one of six state merchant marine academies.

In transportation, jobs involve shift work around the clock. Air traffic controllers work a basic 40-hour week; however, they are assigned to night shifts on a rotating basis. Air traffic controllers work under great stress. They must keep track of several planes at the same time and make certain all pilots receive correct instructions. Pilots work 100 hours a month, but because their schedules are irregular, some actually fly 30 hours while others may fly 90 hours a month. Although flying does not involve much physical effort, the pilot often is subject to mental stress and must be constantly alert and prepared to make decisions quickly. Flight attendants have the opportunity to meet interesting people and to see new places. However, the work can be strenuous and trying. Attendants stand during much of the flight and must remain pleasant and efficient, regardless of how tired from jet lag they may be. Merchant marine officers serve aboard ships. Their duties are hazardous, compared to other industries. At sea, there is always the possibility of injuries from falls, or the danger of fire, collision, or sinking.

Advancement in transportation is usually very clearly determined. In the airlines, opportunities usually depend on seniority established by union contracts. After 5 to 10 years, flight engineers advance on the basis of seniority to co-pilots and, then, after 10 to 20 years, they advance to captains. In other airline jobs, co-pilots may advance to pilots and, in large companies, to chief pilots, who are in charge of aircraft scheduling and flight procedures. Advancement for all new pilots is generally limited to other flying jobs. Advancement opportunities for flight attendants are very limited. Advancement for deck and engine officers in the merchant marine is well-defined and depends primarily upon specific sea experience, passing a Coast Guard examination, and leadership ability.

Transportation offers a great range of opportunities for persons with a college education. Working conditions are generally good and the pay is fairly high. Many employees do a lot of traveling on the job and meet new and interesting people.

AIRLINE PILOT

Flies planes to transport passengers and cargo, to crop-dust, to inspect powerlines and other situations, and to take aerial photographs.

What's It Like to Be a Pilot?

The pilot, called captain by the airlines, operates the controls and performs other necessary tasks for flying a plane, keeping it on course, and landing it safely. The co-pilot is second in command and the flight engineer is third in line to advance to pilot command. The co-pilot, sometimes called first officer, assists the captain in air-to-ground communications, monitoring flight and engine instruments, and operating the controls of the plane. First Officer Charles T. Huggins, Jr., Eastern Airlines, advises young people to get a college education because airlines have not hired pilots without college degrees since 1968. "Then," says Huggins, "get plenty of experience. That means the military. Even though it's a five-year or six-year obligation for pilots, the flying experience in the military is unparalleled to anywhere else. My daily activity includes jogging and exercising because the length of a pilot's career depends upon taking care of himself physically, that is, how long he can hold a Federal Aviation Administration medical certificate." About a pilot's life, Huggins who has two children and is expecting a third says that "a person unable to adjust to a job in which he or she is not home every day would not like it." He was in politics for a while, but then he was never home. His family life is better now. When his 15 work days per month are over, the rest of his time is spent with his family.

Flight Engineer Bob Stephens, married with two elementary school children, likes the everchanging conditions of his work, the travel privileges, good pay, and the freedom away from work because you don't have to take your work home with you. The only thing in his career he doesn't like is the slow advancement to captain. Stephens monitors the operation of the different mechanical and electrical devices aboard the airplane. He checks the weather of the cities on each day's flight route, assists the captain with the flight plan, checks the mechanical condition of the aircraft, and helps the flight attendants check safety equipment.

What Education and Skills Will I Need?

High school: Preparation for college, or technical school, or the military.

College: Most pilots are college graduates and are trained through the United States military service, although they can be trained in flying school. The required 1,500 to 2,000 hours of jet flying time in private lessons necessary to get a job with a major airlines costs more than most students can afford. Most airlines hire flight engineers who are licensed as commercial pilots. Flight engineers work their way up to co-pilot and then to pilot. Pilots must be at least 23 years old and can fly as long as they can pass the required physical examination.

Personal skills: Decision making and accurate judgment under pressure are required skills for pilots.

How Many Pilots Are There and Where Do They Work?

The total pilot population is 815,000, working for scheduled airlines, as teachers, as pilots with business, or for agriculture and government.

$ $ $ $ $

Captains and co-pilots are among the highest paid wage earners in the country. In 1980, starting salaries for flight engineers averaged $14,400 a year. Scheduled airline pilots and co-pilots averaged $67,000 a year flying domestic air transportation, and up to $110,000 a year flying the largest international jets. In 1981, starting salaries for corporate Learjet pilots averaged from $18,000 to $24,000 a year.

What Is the Job Future?

Job opportunities depend on our general economy through the 1980s. Men who get the few jobs available will be college graduates who have experience flying large multiengine aircraft and who have a commercial pilot's license and a flight engineer's license. Many qualified pilots have been put on "furlough" to be called back when needed depending on our energy and traffic control crises.

RELATED CAREER

helicopter pilot

WHERE CAN I GET MORE INFORMATION?

Professional group

Airline Pilots Association, International
1625 Massachusetts Avenue, NW
Washington, D.C. 20036

Local Armed Forces Recruiters

Trade journal

Flying
One Park Avenue
New York, NY 10016

AIR TRAFFIC CONTROLLER

Keeps track of planes flying within an assigned area, and gives pilots instructions that keep planes separated.

What's It Like to Be an Air Traffic Controller?

Depending on the strike situation—chaotic! Air traffic controllers are federal civil service workers. The famous air strike of the summer of 1981 is basically about whether or not federal employees are allowed to strike, even though they must take an oath not to when they begin working. Air traffic controllers' immediate concern is safety, but they also must direct planes efficiently to minimize delays. Some regulate airport traffic; others regulate flights between airports. Relying both on radar and visual observation, they closely monitor each plane and maintain a safe distance between all aircraft, while guiding pilots between the hangar or ramp and the end of the airport's airspace. Air traffic controllers work in a tower near the runway to keep track of planes that are on the ground and in the air nearby. They radio pilots to give them permission to taxi, take off, or land. They must keep track of many planes at once. Airport controllers notify enroute controllers to watch the plane after take off. Each enroute controller is responsible for a certain airspace, for instance, all planes that are 30 to 100 miles north of the airport and flying between 6,000 and 8,000 feet. All commercial planes are under the responsibility of an air traffic controller at all times.

What Education and Skills Will I Need?

High school: Preparation for technical, community, or four-year college.

College: Most air traffic controllers have four years of college before taking the federal civil service exam required to be a controller. After they are selected, controllers are trained on the job. It takes two to three years to become fully qualified.

Personal skills: Speech skills must be perfect and vision correctable to 20-20. A physical exam every year is necessary for this crucial job in air safety. A stable temperament and good judgment are also needed.

How Many Air Traffic Controllers Are There and Where Do They Work?

There are 29,000 air traffic controllers. Most work at the major airports or at air-route traffic control centers near large cities. They are all hired by the Federal Aviation Administration (FAA).

$ $ $ $ $

In 1981, starting salaries for air traffic controller trainees were $12,300 or $15,200 a year. The average salary for experienced controllers was $29,900 a year.

What Is the Job Future?

Very competitive. College graduates who have military or civilian experience as pilots, navigators, or air traffic controllers will have the best chances for work.

AIR TRAFFIC CONTROLLER

RELATED CAREERS

airline radio operator
airplane dispatcher
flight service specialist

WHERE CAN I GET MORE INFORMATION?

Professional group

Dial the toll-free number 1-800-555-1212 for U.S. Civil Service Commission Job Information and ask for the number of the nearest Civil Service Job Information Center, or check your local phone book.

Trade journal

Journal of Air Traffic Control
525 School Street, SW
Washington, D.C. 20024

FLIGHT ATTENDANT

Makes the airline passengers' flight safe, comfortable, and enjoyable.

What's It Like to Be a Flight Attendant?

Before each flight, the flight attendant checks supplies, food, beverages, and emergency gear in the plane's cabin. He greets the passengers, checks their tickets, and helps with coats and luggage, small children, and babies. During the flight he gives safety instructions, sells and serves cocktails, and serves precooked meals. T. Q. Pham, a flight attendant with Eastern Airlines, flies 80 hours a month with 35 hours of ground work duties. He points out to newcomers that all airline jobs with passenger contact have some required shift work. Because the airlines run flights 365 days a year, 24 hours a day, they require their personnel to take turns with this schedule. Planes carry 1 to 10 flight attendants, while 747 jetliners carry as many as 16 attendants. Pham says that what he likes best about his work is the amount of travel and time off compared to other jobs.

What Education and Skills Will I Need?

High school: Preparation for community college, business college, or four-year college.

College: At least two years of college are required by major airlines. The ability to speak a foreign language fluently is essential to be an attendant on an international route.

Physical qualifications: You must be in excellent health, with good voice and vision. You must be at least 19 years old. Even though airlines specify physical attractiveness, you don't have to be "tall, dark, and handsome" to be a flight attendant!

Personal skills: Poised, tactful, and resourceful people are needed in this work to be helpful to the many customers who often are frightened of flying.

How Many Flight Attendants Are There and Where Do They Work?

There are 56,000 flight attendants and most are women, but the numbers of men are increasing. Most attendants are stationed in major cities at the airlines' main bases. College graduates are also in other airline jobs including personnel, customer relations, and marketing departments of management and administration.

$ $ $ $ $

In 1980, the union contracts set the minimum salaries of flight attendants at about $775 to $900 a month for 80 hours of domestic flying time. The major airlines paid an average of $19,000 a year to attendants with experience. Reduced air fare for attendants and their families is an additional benefit of the job.

What Is the Job Future?

Jobs will be competitive through the 1980s. Men with two years of college and work experience with the public will have the best chances for jobs. While in college, take any job working with the public in order to get the work experience you need.

RELATED CAREERS

tour guide
airline ground host
social director

WHERE CAN I GET MORE INFORMATION?

For specific information about qualifications and jobs, write to the particular airlines that interest you. Remember that local and regional airlines may have good opportunities and be less competitive than the national airlines.

Professional group
Air Transport Association of America
1709 New York Avenue, NW
Washington, D.C. 20006

Trade journal
Passenger and Inflight Service
665 LaVille Drive
P.O. Box 507
Miami Springs, FL 33166

MERCHANT MARINE OFFICER

Represents shipowners, directs the navigation and the maintenance of the deck, and supervises the engine department on cargo ships and tankers.

What's It Like to Be a Merchant Marine Officer?

Deck department officers navigate the ship and direct the maintenance of the deck and hull. The chief mate, or first mate, is the captain's key assistant and plans and supervises the loading and unloading of cargo. The chief engineer is responsible for the efficient operation of the engines and other mechanical equipment. He oversees the main power plant and keeps records of the fuel. The radio officer keeps contact with shore and other vessels. The purser does the paper work required for entering and leaving port, assist the passengers, and prepares payrolls.

What Education and Skills Will I Need?

High school: Preparation for nautical science or marine engineering, with a strong mathematics and science background.

College: A four-year program at the United States Merchant Marine Academy or one of the six state merchant marine academies.

Personal skills: Merchant marine officers should have a love of the sea and ship life, which is based on a highly structured social system. They must be able to take orders and live in a small space with the same few people for months at a time.

How Many Merchant Marine Officers Are There and Where Do They Work?

There are 13,000 merchant marine officers. About three-fourths work on freighters and the rest work aboard tankers. Very few work on passenger vessels.

$ $ $ $ $

The money depends on the rank of the officer and the size of the ship. For example, a second mate with a monthly base pay of $2,074 may regularly be increased to $3,110 a month by overtime and extra responsibilities. There are excellent pension and welfare benefits, and vacations range from 80 to 180 days a year.

What Is the Job Future?

Chances for work are excellent for graduates of merchant marine academies. New jobs are being created on research vessels, on ships that carry supplies to offshore oil drilling rigs, and on the dredges operated by the Army Corps of Engineers.

RELATED CAREERS

ship captain
ship master
pilot

WHERE CAN I GET MORE INFORMATION?

Professional group
Office of Maritime Manpower
Maritime Administration
U.S. Department of Commerce
Washington, D.C. 20235

Trade journal
Seaway Review
Harbor Island
Maple City, Postal Station, MI 49664

INDEX OF CAREERS

DESIGN CREDITS

Book design by Edward Smith Design, Inc.

Cover design by Terrence M. Fehr.

Composition in linofilm Baskerville and linofilm Spartan Extra Black Condensed and Spartan Black by Ruttle, Shaw & Wetherill, Philadelphia, PA. Printing and binding by R. R. Donnelley & Sons, Harrisonburg, VA.

PHOTO CREDITS